Giving
HOPE
An Address

Giving
HOPE
An Address

Julie Wilkerson Klose

BL BRIDGE
LOGOS

Newberry, FL 32669

Bridge-Logos

Newberry, FL 32669

Giving Hope An Address: The Teen Challenge Legacy Story
by Julie Wilkerson Klose

Printed in the United States of America

International Standard Book Number: 978-1-61036-472-0

Library of Congress Control Number: 2018931856

Cover and interior design by: Kent Jensen | knail.com

This book is dedicated to my parents
Don and Cindy Wilkerson, for their spiritual
influence in my life.

I am eternally grateful.

Contents

Foreword

By Eric Metaxas

To many Christians—certainly those my age or older—the name David Wilkerson is legendary, as is his now classic book *The Cross and the Switchblade*, which tells the wild and inspiring story of an innocent but fiery country pastor being led by God to what was for him another universe—to the violent gangland world of 1956 New York—and doing things there, or at least letting Jesus do those things through him—that no one thought could be done. But to anyone younger than I, David Wilkerson and the genuinely miraculous story of his ministry to criminals and drug addicts is not much known. I hope this book will change that.

I first had the honor of encountering David and Don Wilkerson in the sanctuary of Times Square Church in the spring of 1990 in New York City. I was just twenty-six and a brand new Christian. Actually what had by then become Times Square Church was for many decades one of the premier theaters on Broadway and is still today a spectacular architectural and cultural landmark. But back in the late Eighties, when Broadway theater was at a particular nadir—from which no one expected it would recover—David Wilkerson and some friends were looking for a place to start a church, right in the middle of the city. So they bought the theater at a great price and turned it into what today is truly the longest running show on Broadway.

I will never forget the worship and prayer that thundered from the first service I attended. I remember thinking as I walked out of the theater and onto the sidewalk that New York could never be the same for me again, now that I had experienced the thunderous praise and worship and faith in that building. It was hard to believe that it existed, right there in the middle of what was then still a crime-riddled and broken city. Something was happening in New York, and from that day on I was hooked and determined to be a part of it. Every chance I got—usually twice per week—I excitedly drove the two-hour roundtrip journey from where I lived in Connecticut to attend another service.

The three pastors at that time—David Wilkerson and his younger brother Don Wilkerson and Pastor Bob Phillips—complemented each other wonderfully, each preaching thrilling sermons, but all in different ways. David was the fiery prophet. Bob was the teacher. And Don—usually my favorite—had an aw-shucks honesty that could often be hilariously funny. I was so affected and moved by their collective ministry that when my second children's book came out—an adaptation of Hans Christian Andersen's "The Emperor's New Clothes"—I dedicated it to the three of them. "For telling it like it is," I wrote, alluding to the message of the book and their boldness in preaching the Gospel in a way I had never heard.

I sent all three pastors copies of the book and was soon contacted by Pastor Don. He wanted me to meet his twenty-four-year old son, Todd, who was at that time interested in writing and drawing. Perhaps I could give the Toddler—as I came to call him—some pointers on publishing. Our meeting led to a friendship and soon afterward I sometimes would stay overnight at their apartment in Manhattan rather than drive all the way back to Connecticut. It must have been at one of those times that I met Todd's sixteen-year-old sister Julie, whom Todd then teased mercilessly, and who grew up to be the author of this book. Of course Todd still teases her mercilessly. He grew up to be a brilliant comic actor, but for his myriad sins has also been condemned to be the announcer on my radio program. But back then we were all practically still just kids, with no idea of what the future would bring.

One weekend at Times Square Church in February of 1994, I hit the Holy Ghost jackpot and met my wife Susanne. After a year of friendship we decided to date and then to marry, and of course we asked Don Wilkerson to perform the ceremony, which he generously did. And of course my friend Todd had to be involved in the ceremony too, so we asked him to read a Scripture passage, provided he promised not to read it in the voice of Walter Brennan ("Aw, Gowan, ye varmint!") or Vinnie Barbarino (Hey Mr. Kotter!")—both of which he does particularly well.

But even if you didn't hang out with Todd, anyone who was in and around Times Square Church over the years would one way or another be drawn into what I must call the "Wilkerson brand" of ministry. They are an extraordinary family who grew up in rural Pennsylvania coal mining country and who were raised in the so-called Holiness Movement, which is a kind of hard-core but movingly authentic Christianity that you rarely see in sophisticated places like Manhattan. There is a fire to their prayers and a passion and joy to their faith that is infectious, and that remains at Times Square Church today, under the capable leadership of David Wilkerson's handpicked successor, my friend Carter Conlon. Today I am privileged even sometimes to preach from that great pulpit where these men I so revere have preached. But for those of you as yet unfamiliar with the soil in which these giants grew, this book tells the story from the inside, so to speak. It fills in a whole lot that *The Cross and the Switchblade* and other subsequent books left out, and it gives you a perspective on Don Wilkerson's singular role in creating Teen Challenge, which has ministered to more drug addicts and alcoholics than we can ever imagine.

I am honored and blessed to know this family and now through this book to know the rest of their profoundly inspiring story of faith in action among the "least of these" in New York City and now, around the world. May it inspire you along the same lines to God's glory.

—Eric Metaxas
New York City
April 2018

Introduction

A Story for a New Generation

"This story has already been told before. Why are you writing this book?" I was asked.

It was a valid question.

In fact, there have been several books written documenting much of this story. I was born in 1973 after this story took place. The faith-based rehabilitation program of Teen Challenge had been established and was a thriving ministry founded by my uncle, David Wilkerson, and my father, Don Wilkerson. At the time of my birth, my dad was the Executive Director of the Teen Challenge center in Brooklyn, New York City, and my uncle was a well-known evangelist traveling worldwide preaching at youth crusades.

The book, *The Cross and the Switchblade*, which documented the beginning of the ministry of Teen Challenge and my uncle's calling to the streets of New York City, was a best-selling book and circulating worldwide in many languages. By 1970, the book was made into a movie starring Pat Boone and Erik Estrada. Teen Challenge was growing and being established in various cities across the United States. Reverend David Wilkerson and the ministry of Teen Challenge were household names in many Christian communities.

Taking a look at the beginning years of Teen Challenge from 1958 to 1973, one could say that I missed the boat. However, I have come to realize that everyone has a story to tell in their own time. This story, in particular, is a part of me even though I was born after its timeline. I am writing behind the scenes giving my perspective for a new generation to testify of God's faithfulness in my family and in the lives of others.

I was raised in a ministry that rehabilitated men and women from drug and alcohol addictions, crime, pornography, prostitution, and sexual addiction. It was not your typical childhood upbringing. I observed people transformed both outwardly and inwardly by the gospel of Jesus Christ. I listened to numerous testimonies of people who were literally on the brink of death because of the powerful control of addiction and watched as they became wholly rehabilitated because they found hope at the address of Teen Challenge. I witnessed broken families restored and understood at a very young age that hope comes from the power of the gospel of Jesus Christ.

Through my research, I came across a newsletter written by my uncle in 1970. President Nixon had just designated thirty million dollars towards an educational program to help combat the nationwide drug epidemic. David Wilkerson wrote, "For the past five years I have been traveling around the country warning people that drug addiction was a national plague. Now this horrible problem has spread like cancer across the entire nation. Everybody is trying to stop it and thousands of 'experts' have suddenly been born. Teen Challenge has been reaching drug addicts for twelve years and has the highest cure rate in the whole world—74% documented. Those who are not cured simply refuse the claims of Christ. No matter what these 'experts' say, there's only one cure—Jesus Christ."

My uncle's words are as relevant and compelling today as they were back then. We are still a nation plagued by drug addiction with the increasing dependency on opioids. In 2016, there were 64,000 overdose deaths with the most increase in deaths attributed to synthetic opioids.[1] It is estimated that more than 90 Americans lose their lives every day due to an opioid overdose. In 2016, President Barack Obama proposed a $1 billion budget[2] to fight drug abuse and overdoses which are at a record high in the United States. In October 2017, President Donald Trump declared the opioid crisis a national public health emergency. Drug addiction is still a cancer reaching all demographics, all races, and all socio-economic communities throughout the country.

This story I am writing is about the same cure that my uncle claimed in 1970. A cure that has a documented success, not because of experts, but because of the testimonies of those who stepped through the doors of Teen Challenge and walked out completely changed. It's about a timeless and sustaining cure that reaps eternal blessings. It's about the power of Jesus Christ.

As a young girl, I remember listening to a chorus of Teen Challenge men singing, men who found freedom from their addictions. They sang a song that captures the theme of my story. They would belt out with loud voices in unison:

I'm a new creation
I'm a brand new man
All things are passed away
I am born again
More than a conqueror
That's who I am
I'm a new creation
I'm a brand new man.[3]

The song comes from 2 Corinthians 5:17, "Therefore, if anyone is in Christ, he is a new creation; the old has gone, the new has come." This Scripture represents the sustaining hope of the ministry of Teen Challenge. It's why this story— today—is still relevant for a new generation plagued by addiction. I have witnessed the role of Scripture in transforming men and women into new creations.

My uncle and my father are the main characters in this book. It is a story of two brothers who were two unlikely people who God used to bring hope to a desperate community. It's a testament to how God uses those ill-equipped to do miraculous things for the kingdom of God. This narrative exemplifies what it means to be a follower of Christ; to love the broken-hearted and share the gospel that brings light into the darkness. (John 12:46)[4]

I am telling a story that began with my family, but it has a legacy that only God can take credit for. You might know these two brothers, or you might be learning about this story for the very first time. I write as a granddaughter, a daughter, a niece, and a woman who has been shaped by a ministry that my family has been privileged to be a part of for sixty years. I am honored to tell a story that began with my family, but I am also humbled by the growing magnitude of this life-changing ministry.

My hope in sharing this story—in my time— is to encourage a family member who is praying for a loved one bound by addiction. It's for those who feel they have lost all hope in finding a cure. I am a voice on these pages telling the truth; that God can use anyone to bring hope to the hopeless. I have witnessed the healing of lives and the mending of families. It has shaped who I am, why I am a follower of Jesus Christ, and why I am writing this book. May you be inspired by this story and may you be encouraged to follow your own calling to bring the hope of Christ to your community.

CHAPTER 1

Rooftop Prayer

1959

"Let's pray that God will give us a place to bring these boys and help them." —David Wilkerson

It was a surreal scene on a rooftop in the South Williamsburg section of Brooklyn, New York, in 1959. A minister from Philipsburg, Pennsylvania and his younger brother found themselves filming drug addicts shooting heroin into their veins. It was to be a documentary film about heroin addicts to bring awareness of drug addiction to churches around the country. No one could have predicted that these two brothers would be using a 16-mm camera to capture a drug epidemic that was taking over the city of New York. They weren't the most likely people to be congregating with drug addicts. In fact, they knew they were out of their comfort zone, but God had plans to use these two men in the city of New York, in ways they could not have predicted for themselves.

MICHAEL FARMER

To set the stage for why these two brothers would find themselves filming drug addicts, we need to back-up to the date of July 30, 1957. For this story begins with the tragic death of a boy named Michael Farmer.

1

Michael Farmer was the oldest of three boys born to Thelma and Raymond Farmer. The family lived in the Washington Heights section of Upper Manhattan, New York City. Raymond Farmer served as a New York City fireman. When Michael was 10-years-old, he became ill with polio and was paralyzed. Doctors did not think he would regain use of his legs, but with intense physical therapy and strong determination, Michael learned to walk again. However, he dragged his right foot and walked with a slight limp physically marking him from the effects of the polio illness.[5]

On the evening of July 30, 1957, Michael and his friend Roger McShane were walking through Highbridge Park in their Washington Heights neighborhood. They were caught in an ambush by two allied gangs: the Egyptian Kings and the Dragons. Juvenile gang violence was at an all-time high during that summer of 1957; eleven murders took place on the Upper West Side of Manhattan carried out by gangs. Teenage gang fights or "jitterbugging," as they called it in the 1950's, was taking place all over the city. Juvenile crime in New York City had risen by 41%, and Police Commissioner Walter Arm remarked about the impact of youth violence, "It's like fighting a forest fire. You don't know where it's going to spring up next."[6]

Michael and Roger were mistaken for Jester gang members and were attacked by the Egyptian Dragons. Roger managed to run away after being severely beaten. Michael Farmer, unable to run due to polio, was beaten and stabbed with a knife and machete. Michael died on that evening of July 30th. He was only 15-years old.

Police caught members of the Egyptian Dragons responsible for Michael Farmer's murder, and their trial made national news. Seven boys, ranging from 15 to 18-years old, were indicted for Farmer's murder. Judge Irwin D. Davidson presided over the trial. In his book, *The Jury is Still Out*, Judge Davidson recalls his first reaction to seeing the boys at the preliminary hearing. "They did not look like killers...from the way they were dressed, most of them came from poor families," he recalls. "As I was to learn later, all but one came from broken homes."[7]

LIFE MAGAZINE

While the Farmer Trial was preceding and making national headlines, David Wilkerson was continuing to pastor his church in Philipsburg, Pennsylvania. It was a growing church located in a rural community made up of hard-working farmers and coal workers. While pastoring, David was becoming spiritually restless. He decided to commit more time to prayer in the evenings and seek God over this feeling of discontentment. It was during one of those late prayer nights in his study that he picked up *Life* magazine. He thumbed through the pages and came across the news story of the Michael Farmer murder trial. There in front of him, David saw the picture of the seven teenage boys appearing before the Judge. He read the horrific murder that was carried out by the gang of boys. He immediately began to cry.

He recalled:

"The story revolted me. It turned my stomach. In our little mountain town such things seemed mercifully unbelievable. That's why I was dumbfounded by a thought that sprang suddenly into my head- full-blown, as though it had come into me from somewhere else. *'Go to New York City and help those boys.'"* [8]

A country preacher, who never had a desire to visit New York City, was suddenly feeling called by God to 'help those boys.' Those boys who were indicted for murder. David couldn't get the idea out of his head, and he knew he had to go right away. He shared his calling with the congregation on the Wednesday night prayer service. The church members heard his passion and honest desire and gave an offering to help pay his travel expenses. The next morning, David and his youth director, Miles Hoover, were on their way to New York City.

BIBLE-WAVING PREACHER

David's objective was to meet the seven boys on trial. He knew the power of prayer and the gospel of Jesus Christ in transforming the lives of those young men. The only problem was the boys were on trial for murder. There was no possible way to gain access to them unless granted by Judge Davidson. It just so happened that the hearing was reconvening the next day at 100 Court Street in Manhattan. David and Miles woke up early the following day and waited in line for limited courtroom seating. They were granted access into the courtroom.

The trial proceeded, and David witnessed the seven boys in person. "I don't know what I'd been expecting. Men, I suppose," he recalls. "These were children. Seven stooped, scared, pale, skinny children on trial for their lives for a merciless killing."[9] David sat listening to the proceedings of the trial when all of a sudden he decided to make his brave move. He grabbed his Bible hoping that it would identify him as a minister and approached the bench.

"Your Honor!" he called out.

"Please, would you respect me as a minister and let me have an audience with you?"[10]

Quickly the Judge motioned the guards and David was picked up by his elbows and pushed out of the courtroom. Judge Davidson, who had been alerted to death threats over this trial, was not taking any chances. He ordered the minister to be removed from the courtroom, immediately.

The Judge later remarked:

"A lean, youngish man with light brown hair and a determined, almost fanatical look in his eye rose suddenly from his seat in the fifth or sixth row and strode down the aisle toward the rope that separated the spectators from the court well. He was brandishing a Bible... He had become deeply absorbed in accounts he had read of the trial and had come to New York to tell us that the whole thing could be solved by prayer."[11]

Minutes later, the press, who were already making this trial a city-wide news phenomenon, questioned David about his intentions in approaching the Judge. They then asked him to hold up the leather-bound book in his hand. Raising up his Bible with one hand, photographers captured a photo of this minister from Pennsylvania that soon spread across every major newspaper in New York City and nationwide.

David and Miles immediately left the city, and David felt like a fool. How would he face his church who sent him on this mission? What would he tell his wife Gwen, when she would see his photograph in the next day's newspaper? Maybe his prayer-time calling was not a divine notion from God.

The next day's news captured David's trial interruption with him holding his Bible outside the courtroom. The New York Daily News' headline read *Bible-Waving Preacher Interrupts Trial.* It told of the courtroom event and David's failed attempt in addressing the Judge on behalf of 'those boys.' The news article ended with the comment, "...it is anticipated that we have heard the last of this poor, misguided heart."

Although perhaps misguided by the world's view, David's heart was still impassioned for those boys and his calling onto the streets of New York City. The questions David mulled over in the days after that shameful courtroom appearance were answered in his continued time of nightly prayer. One Scripture continually came to his mind: "And we know that in all things God works for the good of those who love Him, who have been called according to His purpose." (Romans 8:28) He tried to ignore it. The fact was, as foolish or misguided as it seemed, he knew God was calling him back to New York.

Amazingly, the congregation at Philipsburg Assembly of God Church who financially assisted his first New York City venture graciously supported him again. This time his second trip would reveal God's purpose for why his photo had been spread all over newspapers. Miles accompanied him back into the city. As they drove onto Broadway Avenue, David decided to get out and walk down the street.

"Hey, Davie. Preacher!" he heard shouted in his direction.

"Aren't you the preacher they kicked out of the Michael Farmer trial?" a group of teenage boys asked. They were a part of a gang called the Rebels.

"Yes. How'd you know?" David questioned.

"Your picture was all over the place. Your face is kind of easy to remember."[12]

It was at that moment on that particular street that God revealed to David the Scriptural meaning of 'all things work together for good.'

David's purpose for going to New York City was to 'help those boys' in the Farmer murder trial. He thought he had failed in his cause. Now he realized that although he could not gain access to those particular seven boys, he was identified by the local gangs. In fact, they even called him "one of us."[13] He was kicked out of the courtroom; they were gang members. The cops disliked him; they were disliked by the cops. He was one of them now.

It was all making sense: *Life* magazine, the courtroom photo, the shame, and the persistent notion that he was called to New York City for a purpose. David now had in modern terms "street credit." The infamous event of February 28, 1958, paved the way for David to have access to the gangs in New York. They called him "Preacher Davie" and a new ministry began for him.

Reverend David Wilkerson found his purpose and answer to prayer in this new ministry opportunity on the streets of New York City. But what was going through the minds of Michael Farmer's parents? Here they wanted justice for the death of their son, and this seemingly crazy minister tries to plead for the lives of the boys who were responsible for his murder.

Raymond Farmer later remarked after the verdict that convicted only four out of the seven boys in the death of his son. "My wife and I are not brutal. We don't demand an eye for an eye," he said. "But I thought possibly Michael's death wouldn't be in vain. Now he's a lost cause, an absolutely wasted life."[14]

If only Mr. Farmer could've known this story and how sixty years later his son's death has not been in vain. Unknowingly, the Farmer family would be intrinsically tied to David and the Wilkerson family. God used this tragic death to spark the beginning of what would be a worldwide ministry. What might appear to be unjust on earth may often look different from heaven's point of view. Michael Farmer was not a wasted life.

A FILM AND A PRAYER

A year after that humiliating courtroom event, David found his calling taking him in new directions with his brother Don at his side. He stepped down from his pastorate in Philipsburg to focus full-time on this new ministry. The crime-ridden gangs of New York City were turning over their chains and switchblades for a new kind of thrill. The young men of the 1950's would outgrow the gang life, but the drug problem that was sweeping the country became a habit that many of them could not outgrow. Drug use was becoming drug addiction, much like alcoholism, and was rapidly changing the youth culture.

For nearly a year, David had begun to establish a ministry called Teen Age Evangelism on the streets of New York, bringing the news of salvation and the gospel of Jesus Christ to the gangs. God's calling— to reach the hopeless on the streets of Brooklyn, Manhattan, and the surrounding Burroughs of the city—was becoming a reality. But drug addiction was a new obstacle that both David and his brother Don knew needed to be understood by those outside of the city.

Addiction was not only new territory for the brothers, raised in the quiet country life of Pennsylvania, but this was a scene that few wanted to deal with in the late 1950's and early 1960's. Drug addiction was sweeping across the country, but New York City alone was estimated to have over 100,000 addicts.[15] Teen Age Evangelism had a challenge before them, and David knew people needed to see addiction for the reality it was- back alley or rooftop "junkies" shooting heroin in their veins and desperate for a new high.

With a budget of $102.97, the brothers' objective was to get rare footage of an actual rooftop drug party of addicts shooting drugs into their veins with hypodermic needles. An addict named Shorty led David and Don to a building where they could capture an actual drug "fix." They climbed six flight of stairs to a small enclosure that led to the rooftop which was the stage for the drug injections. With David behind the camera and Don holding the light as steady as he could, Shorty and two other addicts prepared the drug paraphernalia or what addicts called "the works."

Dave then focused the camera on Shorty. The camera zeroed in on a small tin bottle cap held by a hairpin, which was used as the "cooker" to liquefy the drug. Shorty emptied a clear cellophane bag of heroin, placed it in the cooker mixed with water, then lit a match and watched the heroin mixture heat up. As the mixture was cooking, Shorty took off his belt and wrapped it around his upper arm as a tourniquet. Pulling the strap tight, he began to pump his fist, looking for a fresh vein for the injection. Shorty drew blood from his veins in order to mix it with the heroin in the syringe and immediately shot it back into his arm, sending him into a high that he knew would only last for a short while.

All of a sudden, with the needle still in Shorty's arm, David began to faint with the camera tipping over as Don swiftly reached for it before it came crashing down. The three drug addicts quickly injected their veins, all using the same needle, and disappeared while David was passed out cold on the ground. Don immediately began assessing the scene as fast as he could. *Did David capture the drug fix before he fainted? Should he call the police? How would he explain what they were doing and why?* "Preacher Davie's" picture might be plastered all over the newspapers again. Finding the pastor and his brother in the middle of a rooftop drug party might not be so easily explained.

After what seemed like an eternity to Don, David regained consciousness. "The blood, the blood," he stuttered. "The sight of the blood got to me." David was embarrassed and apologetic. "I need to get some fresh air," he told Don. David and Don stepped out onto the rooftop, and David breathed in the fresh air to gain some composure over the feeling of weakness he still felt.

Then David did something so out of the ordinary that Don was taken back with his reaction. David began to cry. With all that happened moments ago in that rooftop enclosure, in a scene that seemed so strange to these two brothers, God began to bring a burden to their hearts for those enslaved to the power of drug addiction. It was very similar to that same reaction he had looking at that photo in Life magazine. Just as he teared up over the faces of those young boys on trial for murder, he was broken over those bound by drug addiction. It was as if his fainting weakness brought about a brokenness before the Lord. "Don, let's pray that God will give us a place to bring these boys and help them," David urged. "We have to do something to help them."

At that moment, David and Don prayed that God would reveal to them how to help those addicted to drugs. They laid out their burden before God, and both brothers felt the urging of the Holy Spirit that a place needed to be established to help those without hope. They knew a home was required to give these young men a new start to find the security to overcome addiction, crime, and be fully rehabilitated.

Their objective that day was to capture rare footage, not seen during that time, of the tragedy and seriousness of the drug problem in the country. However, God seemed to have another plan. He sealed a burden on each of the brothers' hearts that day that would be revealed in different and unique ways throughout their ministry.

The documentary film, called *Teenage Drug Addiction*, shot on that rooftop was eventually completed, and Don's job was to take the video on the road to make people aware of this new ministry and to raise funds. Don, a new graduate from Bible College, had previously been assisting David in various roles in the early stages of the ministry.

The film, although crude by today's standards, achieved what David wanted for this new ministry. He wanted more exposure for a need that few would witness outside the crime-ridden and drug-laden streets of New York City. The burden to help the drug addicted was reaching out to those within the walls of their churches. The prayers and funds of many congregants across the country were instrumental in fulfilling the need and vision for a physical address for the ministry.

The irony of this vision for a rehabilitation home is that Judge Davidson laid out a plan for the city that proposed a very similar type of place. The Judge was emotionally moved by the Michael Farmer murder trial he presided over. He even made a calculated move not to disparage the parents of the convicted boys in hopes that the events that had transpired would bring about change to the families involved. Judge Davidson understood that the boys were from poor, broken homes and many of them were without hope. He never dismissed the boys' evil and ruthless actions, but he had a desire to bring about change for the city in dealing with juvenile gangs.

"It might be discovered that the youth needs a clean, decent home. He needs supervision and guidance twenty-four hours a day. He needs training and work to keep him busy," the Judge said. "In short, he needs a home away from home."[16] The same Judge that dismissed the foolish actions of the 'misguided' minister proposed a similar plan that God was revealing on that rooftop to both the Wilkerson brothers.

It is not known whether Judge Davidson ever knew about David Wilkerson's ministry that was influenced by the Michael Farmer trial, but the irony is rehabilitations homes would be established through a minister kicked out of this Judge's courtroom. Truly, *All things work together for good to those that love God and are called to His purpose.* (Romans 8:28)

If a camera were on those two brothers that day on the rooftop of that Brooklyn tenement, the characters would be two somewhat naïve young men, looking as if they did not quite fit into their surroundings, each bending in prayer with the camera panning out to the panoramic scene of the New York City skyline behind them, both brothers looking rather small in a huge city but feeling an enormous burden for the drug addicted and overwhelmed at the magnitude of the need.

CHAPTER 2

Family Roots

1920-1940's

"I find the day goes much easier if one meets God in the morning." —Kenneth Wilkerson

Some say who we become is directly influenced by our upbringing and surroundings. David and Don's vision for a home to help drug addicts didn't spring up from nowhere. To grow, thrive, and be a sustaining ministry, the vision had to begin with strong roots. The brothers' rooftop prayer—the inspiration that would eventually launch the program—was an example of how both brothers understood the importance of prayer in the workings of ministry and the call of the gospel. They learned the power of prayer from the pastoral ministry of their parents and grandparents.

KENNETH WILKERSON

The brothers came from a family line of ministers; their father, Kenneth, and their grandfather, James Arthur, were both preachers of the gospel of Jesus Christ. Prayer was a central component of their family heritage, and it was also what guided them through life's many struggles. Kenneth Wilkerson had a calling on his life at a young age to follow in his father's pastoral career as a Pentecostal minister. But painful circumstances in his childhood set his life on a different path.

Kenneth and his older sister Gertha did not grow up in a stable family environment. Their father James Arthur, or J.A. as he was nicknamed, was a dedicated minister who often put the work of the Lord ahead of his family. Kenneth and Gertha were sent to boarding school so that J.A. and their mother Della could dedicate themselves full-time to their pastorate position. Gertha and Kenneth felt neglected by their parents and Kenneth would cry himself to sleep at night wanting to be back at home with his mother. "They sincerely believed God required their full attention to preaching the gospel," Kenneth's daughter Ruth writes. "So they willingly made the sacrifice of parting with the children, not realizing the devastating effect their decision would have upon them."[17]

The children would eventually convince their parents that home was where they needed to be and they were no longer sent off to boarding school. However, at the ages of sixteen and eighteen, Kenneth and Gertha would suddenly lose their mother to a deadly infection. J.A. felt the profound loss of his wife and ministry partner. His grief plunged him into his pastoral work while Kenneth and Gertha were forced to grieve alone with an absent father. Within five months of Della's death, J.A. remarried. Gertha married the man she was engaged to and found a new home, but Kenneth would find himself abandoned, once again. J.A. and his new bride, Maxine, made a new life for themselves in a small two-room apartment and together they decided to have Kenneth move in with a church member. Kenneth felt like an orphan and at sixteen joined the Marines to create a new life for himself.

The military gave Kenneth the stability he needed in his life. He distanced himself from his painful childhood upbringing and the Pentecostal faith of his father. He was also embarrassed by the charismatic or holiness teaching that his father preached. Kenneth would often claim he was the son of a Methodist minister, as it seemed more of a respected church upbringing. He rebelled against anything faith-related, and the Marines was the perfect place to experience the worldliness shielded from him as a pastor's son.

As a young Marine sergeant stationed in Cleveland, Ohio, Kenneth spent his off hours drinking, smoking, and enjoying dancing at the local dance halls. Kenneth was a skilled dancer and preferred the dance halls, where he was known for his award-winning dance moves over the local bars. It was in one of those Cleveland dance halls where he met the petite, blond-haired Ann Marton.

ANN MARTON

Ann, the daughter of a Slovakia immigrant family, worked as a secretary in downtown Cleveland. She was a "modern girl" in the 1920's Flapper era with a love of fashion and swing music. She, too, would often spend her nights with friends at dance halls.

On a spring night in 1928, Kenneth entered a dance hall where he spotted young Ann whom he described as "five-foot-two, eyes of blue."[18] Ann was dancing with another man, but Kenneth cut in anyway and before the end of the night was convinced she was not only a great dance partner but that she would be his future bride. Ann was engaged to another gentleman for two years. She was not as quickly smitten with Kenneth but did give him her work address. Not wasting any time, Kenneth met Ann off the streetcar the next morning near her place of work. Three months later, Kenneth convinced Ann to call off her engagement. They married on July 29, 1928.

A FAMILY SECRET

Several months after they were married, Kenneth received new orders relocating him to Quantico, Virginia. Now that he was married and Ann was expecting their first child, Kenneth asked for a release from the military. He wanted to pursue a more suitable career for raising a family. The military did not grant his request. Ann would have to live alone until they gave Kenneth proper release. J.A. and his second wife Maxine offered to let Ann live with them in Hammond, Indiana. Kenneth and J.A.'s relationship was slowly restoring, and J.A.'s offer to Ann helped to build upon their relationship. J.A. advised Kenneth to go to Virginia, and the family would pray that God would grant him a release. Ann moved into the Wilkerson parsonage in Hammond.

It was during this time that Ann learned the family secret that Kenneth kept from her. Kenneth had misinformed Ann and told her that he was a son of a Methodist minister. She was pleased to inform her parents, devout Lutherans, that she was the wife of a respected Methodist minister's son. Ann grew up in the Lutheran denomination and was accustomed to the quiet, liturgical atmosphere of her home church. However, she quickly learned that her father-in-law was not a Methodist but, in fact, he was a Pentecostal minister (or what many people called back then a 'Holy Roller'). Yes, James Arthur Wilkerson encouraged hand raising and spontaneous prayers in his congregation. Ann felt deceived, but she was trapped in this Holy Roller environment while waiting for Kenneth's release.

In time, Ann began to soften her heart toward Kenneth's family and their church. She witnessed their deep love for God, compassion, and she also experienced their passion for praying for the church members. Ann began to grow in her faith and develop a more personal relationship with Christ. She even found herself worshipping God in a new way: with hands raised and outward praise. Ann was excited about this new passion she felt for the things of God and couldn't wait to tell her husband about the change in her life.

Through the prayers of the family and the church congregation, Kenneth received an early release from the Marines. He returned to a wife that was basking in a new faith relationship with God. He witnessed Ann's excitement in her renewed faith and felt a tug on his heart to develop a relationship with God as well. It was the Sunday morning of his return that Kenneth stepped forward to the altar and gave his life entirely to Christ. God answered J.A.'s prayers for his son. Kenneth was stepping away from his old life and towards service to God. He decided to follow his father and become a Pentecostal minister.

THE POWER OF PRAYER

Reverend Kenneth and Ann Wilkerson began a new journey into ministry, but they quickly found themselves experiencing hardships that they hadn't anticipated. Pastoring a congregation during the 1930's and in the middle of the Great Depression meant provisions were scarce. Many times they had to depend on the compassion of neighbors who invited the Wilkerson children to play while providing them lunch or dinner. Kenneth and Ann were learning how to depend on God during an era of financial crisis, a time when church members were struggling to support their families and were unable to support their home church or a pastor's salary adequately. It was during these difficult times that Kenneth and Ann developed a prayer life that sustained them despite their circumstances.

Prayer was the center of the Wilkerson family life in Turtle Creek, Pennsylvania where they raised five children and pastored a small Assemblies of God Church. Devotion to prayer was not only essential to fulfill their pastoral duties but to raise their five children in the knowledge of biblical truth. Juanita, David, Jerry, Ruth, and Donald knew that when their mother called for family prayer time, they needed to stop playing outside and come in. Ruth recalls their family prayers as important times of family togetherness:

> "When the time for prayer came, Mother dispatched the nearest child to round up the others. The entire neighborhood became accustomed to hearing Jerry bellowing out: "Come on home! It's time to pr-a-ay." Immediately we stopped playing and headed for the living room. Our parents never had to explain the importance of prayer. The very fact that it was done daily, without fail, made us respect the sacredness of family prayers. I don't recall one of us refusing to join the family in prayer. I think we all rather cherished these special times because it was one of the few times we prayed as a family…Together we knelt, with the living room sofa and chairs as our altars, and Dad prayed. He called each of us by name before God."[19]

The children witnessed their father's dedicated life to studying the Bible. They were never allowed to play in the house on Thursdays as it was Dad's study time in his second-floor office. Kenneth would often be heard practicing his sermon out loud, and then he would finish his time in prayer. Moans and groans would often be heard as Rev. Wilkerson took his petitions before God. Don remembers running into the house to get a baseball glove and not realizing that his friend followed behind him. His friend looked puzzled and asked, "What's that noise?" Don answered unashamedly, "Oh, that's just my Dad praying." The sound of prayer was as natural and familiar as any other noise in the house.

New ministry opportunities brought a bit more financial security to Kenneth and Ann's growing family. Raising five children and pastoring in a small community in Pennsylvania provided a secure environment where the children witnessed God's faithfulness despite their parents' financial struggles. The family began to experience blessings beyond financial needs. Don, the youngest of the five children, recalls his parents' commitment to Scripture and the compassion they poured out on the congregation they served. "In church, Dad got serious about praying for those who did not know Christ. He added names to a poster to pray for, then as time and prayers passed, and one of those people gave their hearts to the Lord, he would cross their names off the list. I'll never forget watching one person go up to the poster and crossing their name off the list. Dad taught me compassion and to treat all people alike and that all of us are equal at the foot of the cross." Both Kenneth and Ann's compassion for reaching lost souls had a profound effect on their children and would later influence David and Don's calling into ministry.

Church life and family life intertwined in the Wilkerson family. Ministering to the needs of the congregation and working on the various church building projects kept Rev. Wilkerson busy. When the family struggled to meet their financial obligations, the children would be called upon to help out. As teenagers, both David and Jerry worked in a local grocery store to help provide for the family's needed funds. Their jobs didn't leave much room for extra-curricular activities for two teenage boys because the needs of the family took priority.

Even though at times being a part of a pastoral family was difficult, there was also great joy in it. Kenneth and Ann took pride in having all five children involved in the life of the church. The children would often gather together with their mother and father in the family home after the Sunday evening service. These were happy times Don reflected on as "the Wilkerson family jam sessions." It was a real family time of discussion and laughter and a needed release from the demands of church life.

Kenneth's childhood upbringing and the pain of feeling like an orphan made him determined to provide a loving, secure family home for his children. Kenneth and Ann made a choice not to live in a church parsonage provided for them. They owned their house which often made their financial struggles more difficult. Nevertheless, Kenneth felt a family needed an address and a place the family could call their home. It provided a sense of security that Kenneth had longed for in his life.

LEGALISM AND GRACE

The family's Pentecostal upbringing taught them the importance of prayer and the fear of the Lord, but it often tipped the scales toward an atmosphere of legalism. Pentecostal churches, during the 1930's and 1940's, rarely preached grace and mercy for sins and rules were emphasized as a holiness theology. The children were taught to fear God, but it was not uncommon during this new age of Pentecostal revivalism that fearing the Lord meant they were not permitted to take part in activities deemed "worldly." The Wilkerson family household viewed bowling alleys, amusement parks, movies, and even board games played with dice as sinful behavior. The only appropriate social activities were those that centered on the church or neighborhood sports. This legalism set them apart from many of their school friends that were allowed to take part in these types of activities.

This holiness theology had various effects on the five children and their upbringing. Their mother was the enforcer of this doctrine and the working out of one's faith. Don, being the youngest, did not witness the adverse effects of legalism like his older siblings. Like many parents, Kenneth and Ann eventually put less emphasis on rules as they matured both physically and spiritually as parents. By the time Don was a teenager, he was able to enjoy more activities than his older siblings had been allowed to at his age. David, being the second oldest, felt the brunt of this holiness theology in the family. But it was David who secretly took Don to his first amusement park at Kennywood in Pittsburgh, Pennsylvania. Don's brother Jerry took him to his very first professional sports game watching the Pittsburgh Pirates play the Brooklyn Dodgers. David even snuck a TV set up in the attic bedroom he shared with his brother Jerry so they could watch the *Milton Berle Show*.[20]

Each of the five children had to decipher Scripture between God's law and a works theology that did not take into account the grace of God. As parents, Kenneth and Ann defined holiness as not being a part of "worldly" behavior. However, they never ran the household like a prison. They were a family that demonstrated love and the children witnessed the great sacrifices their parents made in creating a happy and healthy home. "Growing up, we stretched the limits of going beyond the legalistic boundaries set by our parents in the household," Don remarked. "But we rarely, if ever, went beyond the biblical boundaries. We somehow knew the difference."

Despite a strict church and family atmosphere, there was no denying that the Wilkerson household had a profound love for the things of God and compassion for those they served. The irony of their legalistic upbringing is that it would eventually lead to a ministry to drug addicts that David and Don would both lead under the banner of God's immeasurable grace and forgiveness of sins. It would be the collision of worldly behavior finding grace and spiritual refuge at an address of hope.

The Christian family that both David and Don grew up in was preparing them for their role in ministry. They witnessed their parents' example of trusting in God through life's struggles, living out the Scripture in Matthew 6:33: "But seek first His kingdom and His righteousness, and all these things will be given to you as well." Their parents taught the brothers to fear the Lord, and, although sometimes this fear translated into a legalistic theology, they understood what it meant to have reverence for God. It gave them a healthy respect and awe for God's power, and it would later provide them with the courage to step out in faith to establish a future ministry together.

David's oldest son Gary writes about the Wilkerson family, "What I can proudly and confidently say about my family—my grandparents, my father, and the heritage they left us—is that they loved God. No one who knew them doubted this. Their hearts were set on Jesus and their gazes were aimed forward, all based on one thing: the faithfulness of the one in whom they believed."[21]

CHAPTER 3

The Call

1940-1958

"God always makes a way for a praying man."
— Kenneth Wilkerson

Like their father and grandfather, David and Don felt a call to ministry. David found his purpose as a young teenager. The Wilkerson family spent their summer vacations at a religious campground called Living Waters Camp in Cherry Tree, Pennsylvania. One particular vacation, David was feeling the insecurities that many adolescents feel. He was very skinny and felt embarrassed by his body. All week during camp, David wore a green corduroy jacket in the heat of summer. He was even more self-conscious surrounded by other boys his age who were more fit and athletic than he was. David awkwardly singled himself out playing sports wearing his jacket.

DAVID'S CALL

It was on the last night of camp, during a message to the youth, that David found a new sense of purpose and security in who he was. The preacher's words mesmerized David and seemed to be directed solely at him:

"I don't care what you look like—your outward appearance doesn't matter to God. It is what is inside that matters. God is looking for young men and women who will love Him with all their heart and mind and faithfully serve His Kingdom on earth... God is calling some young person tonight. He wants to use you to reach thousands of souls for Christ's sake. All He asks of you is that you come and present your body as a living sacrifice for Him. You are never too young to make this consecration to God. Come, give yourself to God."[22]

The significance of those words struck David. God loved him, and he felt a deep love for God. David wanted Christ to use his life for His kingdom. His insecurities didn't define him anymore, his love for God was now his purpose. David jumped up and at the altar raised his hands towards God during the sermon invitation. He prayerfully cried out, "Jesus, use me. Put your hand on my life."[23] A minister put his hands on David's head and prayed that God would use his life for service in God's kingdom. David was overjoyed; he had received "the call."

Kenneth was thrilled that his oldest son had a desire for ministry. He presented David with a book titled *Foxe Book of Martyrs* and gave him some sincere advice: "David, God always makes a way for a praying man. You may never be able to get a college degree, you may never get rich, but God always has and always will make a way for a praying man."[24] Kenneth followed this advice in his life; now, he was imparting it to his children. It was guidance that David would exemplify throughout his life and it would influence those around him especially his younger brother, Donald.

DON'S CALL

Don looked up to David as the older brother. There was an age span of eight years between them. This age difference placed David out on his own preaching and ministering, while Don was still a young teenager occupied with school and sports at home. While growing up in a Christian family, watching his father lead as a pastor and an official in the Assemblies of God denomination, Don grew strong in his faith. He recalls, "I grew up privileged- not financially but spiritually. God had given me parents who were true servants of the Lord, and a heritage of godly role models, including three generations of preachers."[25]

Rev. Kenneth Wilkerson would often introduce Don as the "next preacher in the family." Don never interpreted this introduction as pressure but, rather, an affirmation of what God was calling him to do in his life. He writes, "...I simply assumed since my father said I was going to be a preacher, that it must be so. Later, my heavenly Father confirmed my earthly father's discernment: I was *called* to preach. I am thankful for the seed of God's calling that was planted and nourished by my father."[26]

Don's call was gradual, and it was not a strong pull into the ministry like David's, but more of a feeling that there was nothing else he desired to do with his life. When Don was thirteen, he asked his father how he would know if the ministry was his true profession. His Dad answered, "Whenever learning, studying and understanding God's Word is more important to you than knowing the averages of your favorite baseball team players." This answer wasn't a scolding by Kenneth. His father was instructing Don to desire the things of God over other pleasures in life. After his father's advice, over time Don began to develop a daily prayer life and a passion for seeking God for this direction in his life.

BEHIND THE PULPIT

Their father's dedication to studying Scripture and spending time in prayer influenced both boys to prepare themselves for ministry. David was especially eager to get behind the pulpit. By the age of fourteen, he had already written numerous sermons, and he was anxious to practice his future vocation. David kept begging his father for an opportunity to preach at their church. Finally, at the age of sixteen, Kenneth agreed to let David preach his first sermon at a Sunday evening service. Don remembers the day of David's first sermon: "He boldly went to the platform then clung to the pulpit completely speechless. Fear overcame him. My Dad went up and said to the congregation with a smile 'folks, a little stage fright.' Dad put his hands on David and prayed over him. David started to relax and began to preach, as they say *with fire*, for about fifteen to twenty minutes and the rest is history."

It didn't take long for David to get comfortable behind the pulpit. Kenneth secured other preaching opportunities for his son through various minister friends, and by high school graduation David was ready to enter full-time ministry. His father insisted he get some training first, and David began Bible School in the fall. After one year of Bible training, David took time off to get "into the field" of ministry. His father agreed to this time off to find his niche in ministry life, but he had no idea David would choose ventriloquism as his niche.

David tended to think outside of the box when it came to preaching, which led to his decision to become a ventriloquist evangelist to children. He would travel with his puppet Red, preaching the gospel. David published a pamphlet about Red and would tie the doll to a chair on the roof of his car to attract the children. He drove up and down streets, inviting kids to his meeting. David was a very talented ventriloquist and established himself as a successful children's evangelist in the South.

Both Kenneth and Ann were proud of David's desire to go into ministry, but his eccentric ventures were a concern for both of them. It was a great relief when David decided to take a pastorate position at a small church in Philipsburg, Pennsylvania. He and his wife Gwen and their two young daughters settled into their new ministry at Gospel Tabernacle Church. But David quickly proved that his talents were more directed in evangelism ministry than the more traditional pastoral life.

The church began to grow under Rev. David Wilkerson's preaching. David was a visionary minister, taking a small church and making it flourish with new ministry opportunities. Within two years, David built a larger church on the edge of town. He was also beginning to have a tremendous impact on the youth in the community. He held youth rallies that brought many to Christ. Rev. Wilkerson had transitioned from a child evangelist to a minister preaching to all ages. He viewed each of these evangelistic opportunities as new ways to reach a broader audience for Christ. However, David's passion for ministry was often overly ambitious and, at times, a bit sensational for the 1950's era.

David created the TV program called "The Hour of Deliverance" which aired from the sanctuary of his church. He prominently advertised the TV program's name on the side of his Messerschmitt KR200, an unusual car with three wheels and a glass-dome bubble top.[27] His name "Brother Davie Wilkerson" was displayed underneath the advertisement. David drove the car around town publicizing his show. On the TV hour, he would be announced as the "Evangelist Davie Wilkerson" in a fancy white suit with a sort of celebrity status. People would come from miles around town to be a part of this televised program. He was way ahead of his time before the age of televangelism.

David's showman attitude toward ministry concerned Kenneth and Ann. Don recalls this as a time when "David was trying to be a rock star in the pulpit." David gave his parents their first television so that they would be able to watch his televised program. The TV was kept in the closet as it was considered "worldly" to watch, but they would wheel it out only to view David's show. David would call his dad almost every Sunday night to discuss his program and his ministry in Philipsburg. He was always seeking approval from his parents in spite of his unconventional methods of ministering.

NEVER TOO YOUNG

The church in Philipsburg significantly impacted Don. At the age of sixteen, Don was invited to spend summers ministering with his brother at Gospel Tabernacle. He witnessed his brother's tendency to be a showy evangelist, but Don also saw a passion in David that sought to bring people to Christ and to challenge Christians to draw closer to God.

It was also during this time that Don was impressed by David's devotion to bringing ministry needs before God. Don would watch as his brother walked out into the woods behind the church in the afternoons to spend time with God in prayer. The same dedicated prayer life of their mother and father, witnessed by the brothers, was influencing David's prayer life. Don began to understand the gifts of ministry that God was developing in David, and the unique ways his older brother was able to reach others through these gifts for Christ.

During that summer in Philipsburg, David gave Don his first opportunity to preach during a mid-week service. The same opportunity David's father offered to him at 16 years old, David was now giving to Don and at the same age. This occasion affirmed Don's calling into ministry and created a bond between the brothers. Don began to see David as a father figure, and this relationship would have great significance in their future ministry together.

When Kenneth heard that his youngest son preached his first sermon, he was proud. This event was significant to Don and the ministry calling on his life. Kenneth and Ann were now pastoring at a new church in Scranton, Pennsylvania. Don was allowed to preach from time to time if his dad was away on church business. As the youngest son, he felt the importance of having the opportunity to teach from the pulpit, particularly since he was still in high school. One day, Don received an invitation to speak at a youth rally at another church. "I don't recall what I preached about, but the sermon was titled *Used Car Religion*," Don remembers. "Afterwards, as I left the church an elderly man said, 'Keep it up, young man. Someday you might be a preacher.' All I remember was 'someday.' I thought I already was a preacher! He put a necessary pin in my inflated balloon."

Kenneth encouraged his children to volunteer in ministry at a young age. "Being too young for ministry was never a thought for me," Don recalls. "My father instilled in me Apostle Paul's admonition to young Timothy to let no one disregard youth in ministry (1 Timothy 4:12)." Timothy pastored a large New Testament church despite his young age. Apostle Paul wrote these words to encourage young Timothy. This counsel would prove beneficial in Don's early years ministering alongside David. It was also an opportunity that both brothers would graciously offer to the many young people who would join them in their ministry in New York.

Going to Bible School was the next step for Don in his ministry plans. His dad served on the Board of Directors at Eastern Bible Institute (Now known as University of Valley Forge), a three-year Bible College in Green Lane, Pennsylvania. Don felt this was the most logical place to attend. Having already been behind the pulpit preaching, Don was not quite sure how Bible School would be able to prepare him any more than under his father's mentoring, but Don quickly grew to enjoy his Bible classes and the social life at school. Don recalls one particular time that encouraged his ministry pursuit. "One of the big events at Bible School was that seniors were able to preach in chapel," Don remembers. "They ran out of seniors to preach during my second year and asked second-year students to give the sermon. I was able to speak, and I remember my sermon title was *Therefore Perform the Doing of It*. It was well received with many great comments. Before that sermon, I was just another student, but after that, I was Don— the preacher."

Even though Don became more confident in his preaching abilities, he began to question where his career would lead him. Don recalls expressing to his dad the fear of not finding a place in ministry after he graduated from Bible School. His father counseled him, "Your security is in your calling." He then gave Don the same advice he gave David in his calling into ministry at a young age, "Son, there will always be a place for a man who prays."

God was using both brothers through their ministry roles. While David was venturing into evangelism ministry, Don was feeling encouraged in his dream of one day becoming a pastor like his father. God was directing each brother's ministry talents uniquely. What the brothers didn't know was that God planned on uniting their gifts for a greater purpose.

CHAPTER 4

Losing a Mentor
1958-1960

"If it is of God, it will succeed."   — Kenneth Wilkerson

Kenneth and Ann Wilkerson could not believe what they were reading in their newspaper. A small-town preacher managed to barge into a highly public trial, and that minister was their very own son. Was this another one of David's exuberant forms of evangelism? Kenneth looked at the photograph of his son attached to the newspaper article. David looked scared and naïve holding up his Bible in front of the photographers. He wondered what caused David to take such a risky venture and for what reasoning?

There was a sense of embarrassment surrounding David's courtroom fiasco among the Assemblies of God denomination. Kenneth felt the brunt of the questioning from clergy who felt his son's front page exploit was no more than a showy act by a young and overzealous minister. "Some were understanding," Don remembered. "Many were not, thinking that David had made a fool of himself, a fate they felt should never befall any right-thinking man, especially a minister."[28]

On the way back from New York City, David stopped by his parents' house. He unburdened his heart and the events that led to the newspaper article. David told them of his restless spirit and his commitment to prayer during the weeks before he traveled to New

York. He shared his burden over the *Life* magazine article and for those boys whom he felt God was calling him to reach. Kenneth and Ann began to understand their son's intention despite the disastrous outcome. David was led by prayer. The same commitment to follow God's calling that played out time and time again in the Wilkerson family was playing out in David's life. However, this time it played out in a very dramatic way that no one could have ever predicted. David was merely following God's prompting despite the fact that it seemed to be a failed venture.

ST. NICHOLAS ARENA

The controversy that surrounded David's courtroom appearance quieted down and, even though he was tested, David knew he was acting in obedience to God. In the summer of 1958, David continued pastoring the church in Philipsburg while traveling back and forth to New York City to share the message of Christ with the gangs. David prepared several nights of youth rallies for one particular week that summer to invite the gang members. He booked the crusades in an old boxing arena because no church would allow gang members in their community. The gangs were familiar with the run-down boxing arena. David felt the arena was neutral territory and a better place than a church that might have been an intimidating place for gangs.

On the last night of the youth crusade, Don, who was on vacation from Bible School, decided to travel to New York City for the youth rally. He and his sister Ruth, along with her fiancé, traveled from Scranton, Pennsylvania. They drove into Upper Manhattan to the location of St. Nicholas Arena. Don remembers feeling out of place in an area of the city that few people wanted to venture into from the safe countryside of Pennsylvania.

"We took a seat in the middle of the arena, in the second section. I couldn't help but notice we were the only visitors. A small Spanish choir and a few brave supporters were seated to the left, and right in front of us was a gang! I realized later that these were the 'Mau Mau's,' the gang led by Nicky Cruz and Israel. Scores of 'Chaplains,' Dragons,' 'GGI's,' and other gang members were scattered elsewhere in the seats. I didn't know enough to be scared, but at least I knew I had never seen any evangelistic crusade like that before!"[29]

Don listened that night as David preached an impassioned message to the gang members about the love of Jesus Christ; love that urged the Italian gang members to love the Puerto Rican gangs and encouraged the Puerto Ricans to love those in the Italian gangs. It was a message not well received among those who had physical scars of gang violence. Don felt the hatred in the room. One gang member yelled out towards David, "Hey, preacher! You want me to love the guy that put this bullet hole in my side? Get real, man."

Don saw the disappointment in David's eyes. His message was not breaking through the hatred in the room. David stopped preaching and quietly prayed. Then, miraculously, Don began to witness a complete transformation among those in the arena. David gave an altar call and many of the young men, known in the city as ruthless gang members, began to approach the altar slowly toward the preacher. Hardcore gang leaders like Nicky Cruz of the Mau Mau's were all of a sudden deciding to make a complete change in their lives. Right there, they pledged to give their hearts to God. Many were broken and cried out in prayer. It was a conversion which could only come from the power of the gospel of Jesus Christ. The gang members would later walk out of the arena, holding Bibles in their hands that were given out to them. It was almost too much to comprehend, but knowing that prayer changes things, this turn of events was believable.

THE CROSS AND THE SWITCHBLADE

David later wrote about his work with the gangs and the rally at St. Nicholas Arena in the best-selling book called *The Cross and the Switchblade*. It was his story; a small town preacher who was humiliated outside a courtroom holding his Bible. But through the power of prayer, and following the call of God on his life, David brings the message of Christ to gang members on the streets of New York City. It's the story of a hard-core gang member named Nicky Cruz who only knew the life of crime until he finds new hope in Jesus Christ because of this preacher's willingness to step out of his comfort zone to reach him. This book was instrumental in sharing the call that David was given by God to "go to New York and help those boys." It was a book that captured the attention of a country that was just beginning to understand gang violence and the drug epidemic. It would also highlight the magnitude of drug addiction that would take over the city and spread into the suburbs and across the country.

The book not only told the beginning of David Wilkerson's ministry but was an instrumental tool in sharing the gospel of Jesus Christ. People were intrigued by this story of a country preacher and a New York City gang member. David's son Gary writes, "...what *The Cross and the Switchblade* did so effectively was to report the incredible works of God in the unlikeliest of places, enacted by the unlikeliest vessel."[30] Amazingly, the book resonated with those who had no connection to street life or even drug addiction. It was the theme of hope in the story that brought people to the realization of their need for salvation through Jesus Christ. God miraculously used the book as a tool of evangelism to reach beyond the streets of New York City.

A PIVOTAL MOMENT

The St. Nicholas Arena rally was an amazing night, and Don was able to see it firsthand. Don didn't realize it at the time, but what he witnessed in that arena would be the very spark of a ministry that he and David would begin together. His focus was on Bible School and becoming a preacher like his father, but it was God's providence that he would be at that crusade on that very night. When he traveled back home to his parents, he shared all about David's breakthrough with the gangs and Kenneth remarked, "Just like his grandfather–always doing sensational things."

It was an unexpected, pivotal moment in both Don and David's life. Don looks back at that critical moment,

"When my brother, David, took a risk by faith to share the gospel of love with Nicky Cruz and his friends, he accomplished much more than winning some gang members to Christ. He literally brought the saving message of God's love to a whole new unreached people group, just as William Carey and David Livingstone brought the gospel to unreached people in India

29

GIVING HOPE AN ADDRESS

and Africa respectively more than a century earlier. The big city street gangs of the late 1950's and 60's represented America's most neglected and unreached evangelism frontiers."[31]

David would continually telephone his mother and father to update them on his ministry to the gangs. He was always seeking his dad's approval despite their differences in their approach to ministry. Kenneth often feared that David was "cut from the same cloth" as his father; he leaned toward the sensational things in ministry and had the desire for recognition. However, Kenneth began to realize that his son's calling to New York City was not about making headlines, but about helping troubled youth. He often said about David's ministry in New York City, "If it is of God, it will succeed."

A PROFOUND LOSS

While David was balancing his pastorate position in Philipsburg and his ministry in New York, Don was continuing Bible College. The next event in the brother's lives was unexpected. At the age of fifty-three years old, Reverend Kenneth Wilkerson passed away in February 1960 after battling years of continuous health problems. Kenneth's death was a profound loss in their family. Their father was the anchor that taught them everything about ministry and obedience to the call of Christ. He was the encourager always urging them to live out their calling even in their youth. But above all, their father was their example of a godly man who taught them to put prayer first.

Don was only nineteen years old when his father died. His dream of assisting his father and eventually taking over his father's church in Scranton, Pennsylvania after graduation was cut short. His father's death would be the loss of his mentor. Kenneth would never witness David's full-time ministry to the gangs of New York City, his best-selling book, or the home for those battling drug addiction. David would lose the affirming and approving voice of his father in sharing his ministry dreams. Ann would give up the Scranton church that she and her husband pastored, and the only life she knew as a devoted pastor's wife. Life dramatically changed in the Wilkerson family during the winter of 1960.

Don's future into ministry was linked to his dad. The death of his father would change the direction of his calling and Don began to doubt where God was leading him. He recalls this period in his life,

> "One of the things I came to realize through my father's death was how much my security and calling were tied to my father. The familiar surroundings of a godly family and church had provided a wonderful spiritual environment in which to be nurtured, but I began to question whether or not Christ was at the center of my faith and calling. My heritage did indeed shape my thinking, my Christian walk, and everything about my life, but it was too earthly centered... This was the beginning of my learning that there is more to ministry than preaching, and that the molding and shaping of Christ's character in me was the foundation upon which all ministry and accompanying gifts needed to operate."[32]

Don began to understand what it meant to surrender his future to God. He depended too much on the familiar and comfortable surroundings of his family heritage. Now, God was preparing him, as a young man, to walk out in faith for his future. The affirming words of his father, "Son, your security is in your calling," were more of a reality than ever before.

Both Don and David would continue to follow the call of God in their lives, but each would feel the loss of their earthly father in different ways. Their father's death forged a new relationship between the brothers. Don finished his studies at Bible School uncertain of where God would lead him, but he was ready to serve and to be obedient to the calling on his life. He chose 1 Thessalonians 5:24 as the caption printed under his yearbook picture, "The one who calls you is faithful, and he will do it." Don would learn the real test of that faithfulness through a new call—a phone call from David.

CHAPTER 5

Small Beginnings

1960

"Do not despise these small beginnings, for the Lord rejoices to see the work begin..." —Zechariah 4:10 (NLV)

"Don, I see a revival sweeping across the land with not just kids in the inner-city finding Christ, but suburban youth as well," Dave expressed to Don in a phone conversation. "I am going to need young preachers like yourself to carry out what the Lord has shown me." David telephoned right before Don's graduation and laid out his invitation to help him in his ministry. After five years of pastoring, David transitioned to establishing a full-time ministry on the streets of New York City. He enjoyed his time pastoring the congregation in Philipsburg, but he could not deny the tug on his heart to go to New York. David was reaching the troubled youth in New York City, but he needed help.

Don listened intently to David's request. He reflected upon it, but he questioned whether New York City was his calling too. Since the death of his father, Don was struggling with his future. He was at the end of his ministerial studies at Bible School with no clear direction of where to go. It was a dark time wrapped in uncertainty. He had dreamed of pastoring a church or taking over his father's church. It was a difficult decision to help his brother, and it came at the most inconvenient time. Don felt torn and full of doubt. He was trained to be a pastor and knew nothing about street evangelism. What exactly would this ministry to youth look like on the streets of New York City? Was this project God-inspired or just another one of his brother's overzealous ministry ventures?

David's request challenged Don to rethink just what it meant to be called by God. This was not the calling he had expected. Don anticipated hearing the voice of God tell him where to minister, not the voice of his brother. Even though this call came by telephone rather than some divine direction, Don concluded that God was calling him to assist his brother with this new ministry. Although uneasy about venturing into street evangelism, Don was excited about helping David. He stepped out in faith (to the One who is faithful) and said "yes" to a new challenge. Don recalls, "I sincerely feel that the only reason I did not fulfill this ambition [pastoring a church] was because it was transcended by one that was more important, namely, a fervent desire to be used by the Lord wherever He called me, not merely where I wanted to go."[33]

A PIONEER MINISTRY

As with any new ministry or outreach, the reality of how it begins is rarely glamorous or memorable. Although David reached gang members for Christ and the youth rallies planted seeds for this ministry, the day-to-day reality was difficult and at times depressing. This was evidenced by the bleak three-room office David rented as the site of the ministry headquarters located at 1865 Victory Boulevard in Staten Island. The three-room suite in a less than desirable neighborhood could barely fit three people in a room at one time. Nevertheless, the suite had what they needed at the time: an outer office, an inner office, and a shipping room.

The hardest part of David's ministry transition was that his family was back in Pennsylvania. His wife Gwen and their three small children lived with her parents and planned to move to New York after the school year. In the meantime, David made the small-scale ministry headquarters— complete with a sofa and a hot plate— his temporary residence. It was small and didn't offer many comforts of home, but it was a place that David could commit time in prayer for the needs of the ministry.

It was nearly two years since David had prayed and opened up *Life* magazine. So much had changed for him. He left a thriving church and a comfortable pastoral position for this new venture on the streets of New York City. Now he was living and working in a grubby office suite separated from his family. There was a lack of funds, lack of workers, and a lack of experience in knowing how to help gang members, drug addicts or how to cure the growing drug problem on the streets. He was taking a leap of faith despite the sacrifices. He knew he was called by God to bring the gospel of Jesus Christ to troubled youth. The only thing he knew to do in this process was to keep praying about this new direction.

In July of 1960, five months after Kenneth's death, Ann Wilkerson joined David in his three-room Staten Island office. She knew the demands of pastoring a church on her own were too much to handle. David asked her to join him, and together with Don, the three of them set up headquarters for this new ministry. It was a new adventure for all three of them, and they each had to struggle through with the demands of starting this brand new work. There was no previous ministry, at the time, directly related to street evangelism. It was a new frontier for the three of them that they each felt ill-equipped to handle. It was quite humorous. A newly widowed pastor's wife and her two sons from the hills of Pennsylvania were beginning a street ministry to hardcore gangs and drug addicts demonstrating that God often uses the most ill-equipped people—in unpredictable circumstances— to further His kingdom.

Ann began to feel the strenuous transition of adjusting to life as a widow. She was living in a tiny apartment of her own in an unfamiliar urban environment. Ann threw herself into many hours of work using her secretarial skills from her young single days to get the ministry up and running. What made it more difficult was that David could not pay her a salary until ministry funds increased. Ann quickly began to feel the turmoil of this new and destitute ministry.

FAITH IN THE LITTLE THINGS

Don's job was to manage the tiny shipping room. He mailed out tracts and publications written by David to try and get information out about this new work and drum up support. He was also the designated errand boy; he ran to the store and the bank, and he even got sandwiches on the meager budget that the ministry funds provided. "It was quite a letdown," he remembers. "There I was, an ordained minister, wrapping packages, scurrying to the bank before it closed so I could cash a check for three dollars so we could buy some food to eat that night."[34] Don was beginning to second guess his answer to David's call. This was not the ministry life of preaching impassioned sermons from a pulpit to a welcoming congregation that he had imagined.

Don continued to grow more frustrated with the meager work he was doing. Besides the occasional handing out of tracts and talking to teenagers on the streets, he had very few preaching opportunities. He never complained in front of his brother, but he grumbled about his circumstances to God. "You have called me to this great city and I am even an ordained minister! Why am I working in an office mailing out tracts?" The Lord began to speak to Don's heart, and he remembered the Scripture from Zechariah 4:10: "Do not despise these small beginnings, for the Lord rejoices to see the work begin..." (NLV) Don began to understand what God was revealing to him. God was not calling him to the streets. He wasn't calling him to be successful. He was calling Don to the heart of God; having faith in the little things. It took some time, but Don began to look on these menial ministry tasks as service to God, and God eventually began to answer Don's prayer increasing his responsibilities.

SHARING THE BURDEN

One of Don's first projects that held more significance was the rooftop movie that the brothers filmed together. The street atmosphere had changed drastically in two short years since David first visited New York. The gangs were slowly diminishing because more and more young people were now hustling for money to buy heroin to feed their addiction. Don recalls inquiring about individual gang members that he or David had been witnessing to on the streets. Their friends would mention, "He's not jitterbugging anymore. He's smoking now." Most gang members would begin smoking marijuana and then transition to heroin use. Those who once ran with the gangs were now caught up in the world of heroin addiction, a world that very few, outside the streets of New York City, could comprehend.

David understood that people needed to see this movie capturing drug addiction because if people did not physically see it, it would not be a reality in rural America. Most churches in the United States were only familiar with drug addiction in the form of missionary stories about the opium dens in China and far-off lands. However, David witnessed the devastating effects of drug abuse and felt compelled to warn people that it would soon make its way outside of the city into the suburbs and in their quiet country communities; a prophetic warning that would eventually become headline news stories.

The three addicts that allowed David to film them were the first addicts that Don had met. They were former members of the Hell Burner gang from Brooklyn. David thoroughly explained his purpose in filming them. At that time there was no place, no program, and no strategy to get these young men off drugs except for a few out-patient hospitals. Don recalls David's proposition to the three of them, "If we open a place in Brooklyn where you could get help, would you come?" They eagerly nodded their heads in agreement.

That surreal atmosphere in filming the three addicts, David's fainting spell and then his prayerful plea to God to give them a place to help those enslaved by drug addiction, was all about hope. David saw the hopelessness in these men. He foresaw the growing magnitude of this problem and knew that the hope that could be provided needed an address. The hopelessness burdened both brothers. All they learned growing up in church and watching their father in his ministry was being revealed to them: the power of prayer, compassion for those both physically and emotionally wounded, and the saving power of Jesus Christ in changing lives. But they both knew that hope needed a place, a home, or a facility where love and the power of God could become a life-changing reality in the lives of the drug addicted.

Don was then commissioned to take this twenty-five-minute movie titled *Teen-Age Drug Addiction* on the road to try and raise funds to establish an address of hope. While David and Ann were back in Staten Island manning the ministry's home base, Don was traveling all along the east coast from Florida to Maine.

Roadmaps were Don's constant front-seat companions as he traveled to various churches for the next eight months. He would show the film, churches would give an offering to support this new ministry, and Don would immediately send a money order or check to David to try and cover the ministry's expenses. Don would often receive a letter from his brother at a hotel where he was staying. The letter would be a new request from a church in a different state interested in seeing the film. Churches were responding positively to this new and vital work. The film was accomplishing David's objective in educating people outside New York City about the great need to reach those impacted by drugs. Many people cried after viewing the film and felt the same heart-ache that the two brothers felt. Don recalls two people even fainting at the sight of blood and the heroin "fix." The movie was attracting attention, and people were beginning to understand the devastation caused by drug addiction.

Don was encouraged by the response to the film and the many donations. However, he was growing weary from constant traveling. Every day he went to a new town, new church, and a new hotel. He recalls, "I became increasingly restless. At best, I felt that I was serving the Lord in some roundabout fashion. My desire was to plunge into a more active ministry, but I knew that Mom and David would not be able to keep things going back in New York if I didn't send back the money contributed by those who viewed our movie."[35]

The struggles of this new ministry and its small beginnings were taking its toll on Don both physically and emotionally. Remaining faithful in the little things was proving to be difficult as the ministry struggled and discouragement set in. "I don't want to *talk* about the work. I want to *do* the work," Don explained to his brother after returning from his nearly one-year film promotion.

David began to understand Don's frustration, but he also didn't exactly know the next step for his brother in this ministry and what to do with him. He then decided to release Don to a pastorate position in a small church in Barre, Vermont. David felt Don would gain experience and maturity pastoring a congregation. So Don packed his car and headed to Vermont leaving New York City behind him. He left behind all the challenges of this struggling ministry: all the miles logged promoting this work, and the prayer to establish an address to help those lost in drug addiction. Maybe the streets of New York City weren't his calling after all. Don was ready to move on and step behind the pulpit.

CHAPTER 6

The Birth, Death, and Resurrection of a Vision

1960-1961

"This is the place. This is the place God wants for us."
—Harald Bredesen

Don's acceptance of a pastorate position in Barre, Vermont wasn't happenstance. In fact, it was quite convenient since his fiancée, Cynthia Hudson, grew up in the small nearby town of Plainfield.

Don had met Cindy at Eastern Bible Institute in Pennsylvania. In his second year, he caught a glimpse of a pretty young woman in a red dress walking toward the dining hall. Cindy was a first-year student, and Don awkwardly tried to make a comment to get her attention. He failed, but later he managed to get enough nerve to ask her to join him on a walk "down the lane." To his surprise, she agreed. The lane was the only place on campus that men and women were allowed to socialize one on one, albeit with some distance between them. It was during these walks that Don began to get to know Cindy, and he became attracted to her gentle and quiet spirit. "She stood out to me because of her innocence and her sincerity," he recalls. "She was the first young lady I knew outside my own denomination of The Assemblies of God, and I was curious why she came to Bible School."

Cindy attended the Methodist church in her hometown of Plainfield. Growing up, Cindy went to church regularly. As a young adult, on one particular evening, she attended a special revival service at her church. It was at the revival where Cindy made a life commitment to Christ and had a new passion for the things of God. She wanted to know more about serving God and desired to learn more about the Bible. Her desire to know more of Christ sparked her interest in attending Bible School. She worked two years in an Insurance Company as a secretary while putting money aside to attend Eastern Bible Institute in Green Lane, Pennsylvania.

Don's upbringing in the Assemblies of God church and his spiritual heritage was opposite of Cindy's childhood. Don began to appreciate Cindy's yearning to know more about God and her genuine interest to grow in her new faith. "The typical male student preparing for ministry was interested in a future wife who could do many of the following: play piano, sing, teach children, and come from a church background with good connections. Cindy was none of the above and was not the typical candidate for a future pastor's wife, but our daily walks down the lane confirmed to me that she was 'the one.'"

While Don had been traveling all across the east coast promoting the film for the new ministry work in New York, he looked forward to the many letters that Cindy sent while they were apart. The letters were the highlight of those days that were often long and lonesome. Don and Cindy's courtship through Bible School and, later, their letter correspondence confirmed what they both felt; God was leading them to marriage. As they planned their upcoming wedding, the pastorate position in Barre seemed like the next step for Don.

"Dave, I have accepted the job at Barre," Don telephoned David to tell him the news.

(Silence.)

"Dave, are you still there?"

David questioned, "How many members?"

"Six."

(Silence)

"How much are they paying you?"

(Long pause.)

"Nothing."

David questioned Don again, "Are you sure you know what you are doing?"[36]

This new position wasn't the most financially appealing of prospects, but Don didn't hesitate when all six church members unanimously voted him in. He was 21 years-old and accepted his first pastoral position. Don sensed that, despite the drawbacks, this was where God wanted him. The ministry in New York City was changing from working with gangs to helping drug addicts. There was uncertainty about the future of the work and its direction. Ann Wilkerson encouraged her youngest son to take the new position in Vermont. She witnessed the differences between David and Don and feared that they would clash and tensions would rise as the ministry grew. Don was ready for this new calling and his future life with Cindy, his bride-to-be.

PURSUING THE DREAM

While Don was settling into his new pastorate position, David was struggling to make his dream of a home for drug addicts a reality. The ministry was stumbling along, and David was trying everything to raise enough funds to keep it going. He first put all his energy into a literature campaign reaching teens in the inner-city schools and tackling subjects like drug addiction, sex, and gang violence. He wrote pamphlets and tracts offering help through the Bible and the love of God. There were eye-catching pill capsules, and even a fake cigarette box with a series of tracts inside that shared the gospel. Unfortunately, the tracts and pamphlets were reaching very few teenagers with few results.

He then turned to television, like his previous pastorate days in Philipsburg. He hosted a weekly 15-minute television program featuring a youth choir along with testimonies from former gang members and drug addicts. The television series was popular among the teenagers of the city, but after the first thirteen weeks the cost and debt that accrued outweighed the results. David also began to feel that something was missing in his ministering and promoting of this new ministry. He started to go back out on the streets and talk face-to-face with the young men and women. God was reminding him of the very first days when he ventured out into the city, unsure of how and why God was leading him there, but he would share his burden and his heart with gang members. He realized he was departing from the core of this ministry—personal evangelism.

"I knew that I had touched the live, vital key to effective work with people. Jesus did not have television or the printed word to help Him. His was a face-to-face ministry. I knew that as soon as I returned to my original technique of going out into the streets that this was the method meant for me...but the more successful my experiences on the street, the more I realized that we had to act on the problem of follow-up. With most of the youngsters I was satisfied if I got them established in a good local church. But with the boys who were in serious trouble, or had no home, some closer form of follow-up was needed."[37]

One day, after stepping off the ferryboat from Staten Island, David got on the subway and headed to Brooklyn to spend time talking to people on the streets. While hearing the roar of the subway on the tracks, David suddenly thought back to his original dream of a house located in Brooklyn. This time the name of the place came to him. The home would be called *Teen Challenge*. David began to envision this place of hope located in one of the roughest parts of the city.

"There, in Teen Challenge Center, we would create an atmosphere that was so charged with this same renewing love I had watched on the streets, that to walk inside would be to know that something was afoot. And here we could bring boys and girls who needed special help. They would live in an atmosphere of discipline and affection. They would participate in our worship and in our study. They would watch Christians living together, working together; and they would be put to work

41

themselves. It would be an induction center, where they were prepared for the life of the spirit."[38]

After almost a year working full-time in the city, David began to actively pursue the dream of opening the Teen Challenge Center. There was one major problem. He had no money to buy a place. He discussed his need with local churches. He also preached and raised funds to help meet the need. The financial burden of pursuing this venture weighed heavy on his mind. It took the prompting of his wife Gwen to help him to begin to step out in faith. "You're trying to raise your money first, and then buy your home, she said. "If you're doing this in faith, you should commit yourself to your Center first, David, then raise your money for it."[39]

After Gwen's prompting, David began to trust in God's plan as he committed in prayer his dream of a home for gang members and drug addicts. On December 15, 1960, while praying in the early morning hours, David felt that the home should be in the crime-ridden area of Bedford-Stuyvesant, Brooklyn. He then located the exact street where he felt God was leading him to buy a house. He circled Clinton Avenue, the future home of Teen Challenge Center.

Clinton Avenue was located in the Clinton Hill section of Brooklyn. The neighborhood was established in the early 1900's, situated on a hill that overlooked the Hudson River and the island of Manhattan. Many of the wealthy in Manhattan moved out to the farmlands of Brooklyn and built stately brick mansions along Clinton Avenue. They built their summer homes along cobblestone streets where commercial traffic was not permitted. This provided a quiet reprieve from the hustle and bustle of Manhattan. It was an area of Brooklyn that was once the hub of wealth and prosperity. The Clinton Hill section in 1960 was very different from what was once prime real estate of New York City. Many of the stately mansions were run down with crime and poverty overtaking this section of Brooklyn.

With a $125.73 balance in the ministry's bank account, David began to look at some houses for sale on Clinton Avenue with a few members of the ministry's Board. Each building they visited began to go up in price as the bank account balance began to decrease. David's lack of money was proof that he was stepping out in faith.

"This is the place. This is the place God wants for us,"[40] Harald Bredesen, a Board member, remarked as they entered a stately, red-brick, Georgian house. It was the most expensive and run-down house they had visited. David was not impressed as he describes:

> "Never have I seen such a shambles. The house had been unoccupied for two years. For several years before that, students from a nearby college had used it for a combination clandestine flophouse and brothel. An old recluse lived in the house now, illegally. He was one of these old men who finds his security in accumulated junk, and he filled every room in the house with newspapers, broken bottles, skeleton umbrellas, baby carriages and rags... Most of the water pipes were broken, plaster fell from the ceilings and walls, banisters lolled on their side and doors were ripped from their hinges."[41]

The owners of the house were asking a price of $65,000, but they brought the price down to $42,000 dollars in negotiations due to the amount of work that was needed to restore the home. The price didn't seem like a bargain with only a hundred dollars in the bank. David knew the tremendous amount of labor that would be required to make the house livable. He wanted to provide a welcoming address where men could feel the security of a home. It was his adamant desire to give hope to the men and women he was ministering to out on the streets. This home would also house Christian workers to assist those found on the streets, providing for their emotional needs and to help them overcome their addictions. Unfortunately, the financial requirements of purchasing this home and the amount of work that would have to go into it seemed overwhelming. Was 416 Clinton Avenue the address God wanted for the Teen Challenge Center? David did what he always did in times of need. He brought it to God in prayer, knowing that if this was the home God intended for Teen Challenge, it would come to fruition.

THE MIRACULOUS PURCHASE

If the address of 416 Clinton Avenue was the will of God, then, like Gideon in the Bible, David would put out a fleece before God. To purchase the building, he would need to raise a ten percent down payment of $4,200, and he would need it in one week. He had an upcoming speaking engagement to make an appeal at a local church called Glad Tidings. The timing of the request was terrible. Not only did he need the down payment for the house in one week, but the request opportunity came in December, right before Christmas. By faith, David laid out his request in prayer before God:

> "Lord, if You want us to have that building, You can let us know for sure by allowing us to raise that in a single afternoon. And furthermore, Lord, let me raise that amount without mentioning how much we need. And furthermore, let me raise it without making an appeal. Let this be something the people do out of their own hearts."[42]

Miraculously, the congregation of Glad Tidings answered his three-step prayer. Widows, school teachers, and individuals who did not have much to offer gave what they could because they felt led by God to give to this pioneer ministry. There was no Christian organization like Teen Challenge at the time, and they understood the need for a place where David could share the love of Christ to those struggling with addictions. Not only did the people of the congregation give to the building fund, but they gave over and above, $4,400 dollars. David questioned why God would allow the extra $200 when only $4,200 was needed. On the day of handing over the check to the lawyer in the amount of the $4,200 down payment, the lawyer reluctantly explained that there would be some unexpected fees to pay the lawyers. "How much money?" David asked. "Two hundred dollars," they replied.[43]

God answered and exceeded all expectations, supplying every need for the purchase of 416 Clinton Avenue. Once again, David trusted and believed, and God answered. This would be one of many times when God provided funds through faithful believers for the ministry of Teen Challenge. It's through God's faithfulness and countless people that Teen Challenge could open and run at its first address. David's dream of opening a home was a reality. This home was purchased in prayer by faith. These two themes—prayer and faith—have been the cornerstones of the Teen Challenge ministry.

A STRUGGLING PASTOR

As David put his trust in God toward the purchase of Teen Challenge Center, Don was miles away and too busy trying to make a living and pastoring a church with his new bride to think of the work in New York. Although the church did not pay a salary, they did provide Don and Cindy with a small apartment on the second floor of a house near the church. To make ends meet, Cindy worked as a secretary at an Insurance Company in the nearby town of Montpelier. Don took a part-time job as a tour guide at Rock of Ages, a large granite quarry that made tombstones and monuments.

Along with Cindy's full-time job and Don's part-time work, they also worked to promote and pastor their small congregation. At their Sunday morning services, there were only about a dozen people in attendance. Their Sunday evening and mid-week services consisted of the faithful five: four senior women and an older gentleman who often dozed off during the middle of Don's sermons. Calling the congregation small was an understatement. Don felt discouraged by the lack of growth in the church despite their evangelistic efforts to invite newcomers. He was eventually laid off from the quarry job as guides were unnecessary during the winter months. Don struggled to find employment in an area where jobs were scarce. He was able to provide some income working as a part-time grocery clerk. Newly married and unemployed, Don realized the challenges of ministry and the financial difficulties of making a life with his new bride. If God was teaching him maturity and experience, then he certainly felt the full impact of it.

Don's vision of working with his brother helping drug addicts and providing them a home was a distant memory. It was hard to visualize any ministry when working as a grocery bagger transferring groceries to a shopper's vehicle. Don felt humiliated by his role as a struggling pastor having to preach to less than a dozen congregants a week, and scarcely being able to get food on the table for both him and Cindy. Don's repeated life lesson of being faithful in the little things was becoming increasingly more difficult to understand. His calling— sparked by God— now seemed to be burnt out.

A LESSON FROM GRIEF

Despite the financial struggles in their first year of marriage, Don and Cindy were pleasantly surprised when they found out they were expecting their first child. Even with all the uncertainties, they both found joy in anticipating the birth of a baby. Cindy worked through much of her pregnancy which became difficult to do as she was extremely sick from the very beginning. She was relieved when in her seventh month of pregnancy she was not permitted to work due to company policies. Cindy was able to collect unemployment compensation while resting at home.

In January, late in her pregnancy, Cindy was rushed to the hospital with a great deal of pain. Don anxiously awaited word from the doctor. "Your wife is fine, Mr. Wilkerson, but your baby girl was stillborn," the doctor explained. Don and Cindy were overwhelmed with grief at the loss of their first child. Cindy remembers the piercing pain of losing the baby and lying in the wing of the hospital watching nurses carry newborn babies to their mothers' bedsides. Mothers embraced their babies with joy while Cindy was racked with grief. "Why, Lord? Why do we have to go through this?" Cindy cried out to God. The challenges of a difficult year and the death of a child seemed too much to endure. While family members were visiting new mothers and their babies, Cindy's family was helping her with burial arrangements for her first child. She chose the best dress out of her new baby purchases for the burial, and Valerie Wilkerson was placed in a small grave in Cindy's hometown.

Don and Cindy's first year of marriage was very long and challenging for the both of them, but the death of Valerie made it that much harder. It was a year of life lessons to learn as followers of Christ. The humiliation of financial struggles and the pain of losing their first child were preparing them for their life work in ministry. They didn't know it at the time, but that first year would help them to identify with those who also felt pain, struggles, and feelings of failure, especially in the work of ministry. God was preparing Don and Cindy for their ultimate life's work—Teen Challenge.

A RESURRECTED CALLING

"Don, the work has grown tremendously in the past several months, and I need your assistance," David urged Don. "I need someone who not only understands the nature of this work but someone I can completely trust and depend upon... It won't be easy for you and Cindy, but the challenge is here waiting for you to accept it."

It was a letter of encouragement from David and arrived at just the right time after a long and painful year for Don and Cindy. David asked Don to return to the ministry in New York. Don felt a renewed calling, but Cindy hesitated. She didn't want to take the easy way out of a challenging year. She didn't want to run away from their hardships unless God was, indeed, calling them. Cindy also didn't want to leave their small congregation without a pastor. They both knew that if New York City was where God was leading them, then God would have to answer their prayer to bring in a new pastor for their small congregation. Don and Cindy laughed in disbelief, knowing the chances of any minister wanting to take on a small congregation without a salary was unlikely. Amazingly, within a few weeks, a visiting minister knocked on Don and Cindy's apartment door unexpectedly. The minister inquired on behalf of a young pastor who was looking for a small church he could take over. He was a young man who owned his own business and was financially secure, allowing him to transition as the church's minister easily. God answered their prayer. Off they went to New York City.

Don and Cindy would later look back on that first year and see God's faithfulness. Don recalls his father telling him to be a good listener and learn from every experience. It was a year of many difficult experiences. Now they were leaving their small congregation and the small community of Vermont for the streets of New York City. They were moving on and trusting God, even with all the uncertainty in this new ministry. It was almost precisely a year to the day that Don left his brother to pastor the church in Vermont. Now with Cindy by his side, he returned to the ministry that God initially called him to. A vision resurrected.

CHAPTER 7

416

1961-1962

"We believe in the total cure of the total man! Only God can grant that kind of cure."
                                        —David Wilkerson

Before Don and Cindy arrived at the doorstep of 416, much had transpired. David and many volunteers had been busy with preparing and opening the Teen Challenge Center. The first major obstacle was cleaning up the building. The house had been overtaken by years of accumulated junk. It took six Sanitation Department trucks to haul everything away and clear the rooms. Next came the necessary repairs to the building: a brand new sprinkler system, newly painted walls, and furnished rooms. This was all achieved with the generous donations from many churches and donors who heard of Teen Challenge and believed in its vision.

Finding enough money to open the center was challenging in those early months. David felt the financial burden of restoring and running the center. He would spend the money as soon as he raised funds leaving only a few dollars in the bank account. David began to understand God's lesson in his financial difficulties.

"Often I've yearned for a financial situation that would allow us to breathe a little more easily. But just as often, I come back to the conviction that the Lord wants us to live this way. It is one of the most demanding requirements of our faith to depend totally on God for the needs of His work. Just as soon as we have a balance in the bank, we'll stop depending on Him in the day-to-day, hour-by-hour way that we now do, not only for our spiritual needs, but for our physical needs as well."[44]

The clean-up and restoration of the 416 Clinton Avenue building would become a metaphor for the Teen Challenge program. David knew that the gospel of Jesus Christ could clean-up the lives of those he met out on the streets. He witnessed miraculous life transformations like former gang leader, Nicky Cruz, who gave up gang life to serve God in full-time ministry. David believed in the cure of addiction through Jesus Christ. The physical restoration at 416 would provide both spiritual and emotional rehabilitation for those who walked through the doors of the center; restoring this run-down home with an end-goal of repairing broken lives. The home was a real representation of David's vision, but it took faith to achieve.

STREET EVANGELISM

Mike and Kay Zello remember living entirely by faith in the summer of 1961 when Teen Challenge first opened its doors. Mike Zello met David Wilkerson in 1958 when he was a seventeen-year-old living in Brooklyn. He knew, all too well, the violence of the gangs in his neighborhood. His family was forced to move out of the Fort Greene area (that encompassed Clinton Avenue) because of the crime and danger of the gangs. David invited Mike to work with him on the streets and minister to the same gangs which drove his family out. David often asked teenagers and any young person willing and available to help. "Nobody wanted to work with David in the early days," Mike remembers. "Churches received him to hear him speak but few people were willing to go out on the streets with him." David began to travel to Bible colleges to recruit students to work with him out on the streets during the summer months.

Kay Ware Zello was also one of the first recruits in the summer of 1961. She was an eager student at Central Bible College whose sole desire was to be used by God. She recalls Rev. David Wilkerson coming to speak at one of their Friday night chapels in the early spring. "His message was unlike anything we had ever heard before as he shared his burden and calling to the streets of New York City." Kay, along with many other students, felt compelled to go and take part in this brand new ministry. At the same time, David was realistic with them. He painted a dark picture of crime, gangs, and danger, unlike anything these students had ever experienced. Pastor Wilkerson advised that this ministry would be a test of their faith. It would be a week by week dependency on God to meet their needs both spiritually and physically. "I cannot promise you anything but a bed to sleep on, and we'll believe God for the rest," she recalls David challenging. Many students decided not to go, but Kay, along with a team of others from Central Bible College and Lee University, trusted God for protection and traveled to New York City.

The house at 416 Clinton Avenue would eventually take in former gang members and recovering addicts, but in its early days its use was to house the teams of young Bible students. These students would go out with Rev. Wilkerson to the roughest parts of the city sharing the gospel of Jesus Christ. If the address at 416 was going to offer people the hope of Jesus Christ, then they would need to know where to find this hope. The teams of students would take that message of hope into some of the most dangerous neighborhoods in the city, places like Little Korea in the Bronx, Red Hook in Brooklyn, and Harlem in Manhattan.

David understood that to reach the gangs and addicts he would have to minister to their spiritual needs before their physical needs. However, he would not be able to get them in a church building. So he took the church out into the streets, into the most dangerous neighborhoods, and met them where they lived and hung out. It became evident that the tool of David's vision for Teen Challenge was street evangelism.

Each morning the teams of young people would get up, have a time of prayer in a chapel service, and have lunch. The groups would then go out into various neighborhoods in the city while passing out evangelism literature and sharing their testimonies about the transforming message of the gospel of Jesus Christ. They would invite people to attend the evening rally where Rev. Wilkerson would speak from a makeshift platform on a street corner or a local park. Kay remembers those early days on the streets. "There is no way to convey to you the sovereign way that God brought together a group of young Bible School students who were completely sold out to Jesus. We were ready to lay it all down and die on the streets of Harlem if necessary, to reach these gang members that Dave was called to reach. We were willing to sacrifice anything, pray as long as he wanted us to pray, and go out on the streets and stay as long as he wanted us to stay, and we went to some really rough places."

Many times the teams that went out were viewed with hostility and not welcomed. Mike recalls one meeting where someone was throwing eggs at them from a building. David encouraged them to be friendly but persistent. Eventually, the gang members and people of the neighborhood grew accustomed to their regular visits, and many looked forward to seeing them. Gradually the teams began to build relationships with people in the communities.

One humorous aspect of that particular summer was that many of the young Bible students had never set foot in a big city like New York. Many were from hometowns in the Mid-West, and they would smile at people on the subway and make eye contact. Mike, a Brooklynite, recalls questioning David, "You have all these kids here, and they don't even know how to act in New York City." David responded, "Shhh, don't tell them." That first team of workers might not have had street smarts, but they had Bible knowledge. David knew they would be able to evangelize and share the message of the hope of Christ out on the streets. The reality was that David had much in common with these naïve students. David or "Pastor Dave" as many called him, stuck out as a "hick from Pennsylvania." He often would try to use street lingo to sound cool among the gangs, but he used it in the wrong context. However, those working with Pastor Dave could see past his awkward ways. "But we all knew he was sincere. We saw his heart and his passion, and we were drawn to it," Mike shared. Just like the students, what David lacked in street smarts, he made up for by his gift of personal evangelism.

THE POSITIVE CURE FOR ADDICTION

The importance of including the local church was instrumental in David's evangelistic outreach. His goal was to take the new converts who made decisions for Christ at the rallies and plug them into a church in their neighborhood. The intention was for these churches to follow up with these young converts, but many churches were not equipped to know how to reach these former gang members or those who were dealing with drug or sexual addictions.

It was evident that the Teen Challenge Center needed to make the transition to welcoming those who needed a full-time home for rehabilitation and discipleship. The gangs were diminishing, and teens were turning to heroin rather than fighting in the streets. The Teen Challenge Center was transitioning into a permanent place of offering hope in a time where drug addiction seemed hopeless or without a cure.

Drug addiction spread beyond comprehension during the 1960's. By 1962 heroin use was growing fast in the major cities of the United States. No one understood how to deal with drug addiction effectively. Medical institutions would treat the addict, but relapse was statistically evident. In 1962, President John F. Kennedy spoke at a conference on narcotics and drug abuse. He remarked, "I don't think that there is any field about which there is so much divided opinion, so much possible to do, and, in some places, so limited in action as this field of narcotics and drug control of abuse...The discouragingly high degree of relapse among addicts who leave our medical institutions free of any physical dependence on drugs is clear evidence that more must be done."[45]

While representatives from various Federal agencies, law enforcement, and fields of medicine were gathered at the White House to solve the problem of the growing drug epidemic, the house at 416 Clinton Avenue was establishing itself as a place to rehabilitate those struggling with substance abuse. David Wilkerson's success was due to his knowledge that addiction was first a spiritual problem. At 416, God would meet you at the door. To be fully cured, the addict is introduced to Christ, and restoration follows. It was called the "positive cure for drug addiction," and it was presented in a literature track written by David that many of the Bible students would hand out on the streets.

David responded to President Kennedy's challenge on the drug crisis:

> "Teen Challenge is a faith-based program that has accepted the late president's challenge. It is a unique program that offers undeniable proof that drug addiction is a spiritual problem that can be solved only by the power of God! Teen Challenge is not interested in just curing the addict of a drug habit. We believe the addict is not fully cured until he has the power within himself to conquer all his habits. He is not cured until he is fully motivated to work and to stand on his own two feet anywhere and in any crisis. He is not fully cured until he makes restitution for his past wrongs. We believe in the total cure of the total man! Only God can grant that kind of cure."[46]

A PLACE FOR ALL AGES

The one aspect of Teen Challenge that needed to be addressed was the word "teen" in Teen Challenge. When David started to minister out on the streets of New York City, he was mostly talking to young people because the gangs of New York were mostly made up of teenagers. After all, it was the young teenage boys in Life magazine that first caught his attention. He had wanted to focus his ministry on a select group, but over time that changed with the influx of drug addicts. Many of the young Bible School students ministering on the streets found that those who needed help were older than them. David realized that the residential center at 416 Clinton Avenue had to focus its attention on both teenagers and adults. A 43-year-old drug addict named George Callen who was helped through the Teen Challenge program responded to the programs name, "It doesn't matter what you call it. This is a place where God works on everybody."[47]

The news of Teen Challenge was spreading. Christian Herald magazine had featured David documenting his courtroom appearance and his work with gang members like Nicky Cruz. More people began to understand how violence and drug addiction were impacting the city of New York. Teen Challenge was putting a face to gang violence and drug addiction. People throughout the country were starting to realize that the Christ response to addiction was not only an effective form of treatment, but it was restoring broken lives of all ages with proven results. The ministry was still struggling along financially, but David knew that God had raised up this ministry for a purpose. Rev. Wilkerson was determined to start this ministry, and he had the confidence and faith to keep it going. "I know God has raised this ministry," he confirmed. "If we lose this building, I am going to walk down the street and buy another one."

In the Spring of 1962, Don and Cindy drove from Vermont through the city streets of New York in search of 416 Clinton Avenue. They had no idea what to expect as they searched for this address, but, from the look of the run-down buildings along the streets of Fort Greene, Don and Cindy began to realize the magnitude of this ministry. "There it is, Don!"[48] Cindy pointed out as she read the number 416 on the newly painted white door. They saw a four-story red brick colonial house standing out amid two shabby looking apartment buildings. The house had freshly painted white trim on its windows and shiny green ivy growing along the front of the building. It was surrounded by an old iron fence noting its early 1900's history as a stately mansion. The house was a welcoming sight in such a run-down area of Brooklyn.

Inside, Dave warmly welcomed his brother and sister-in-law to 416 and began to tell them about all the restoration work on the house and how the ministry had grown within just a year's time. It was exciting to hear about the street ministry teams and how the center was now beginning to work full-time to rehabilitate those of all ages with drug addictions. Don started to feel the excitement of this ministry. It wasn't very long ago that he and his brother had committed to God in prayer on that rooftop in Brooklyn for this very place. Now he and Cindy were walking through the halls and rooms of what was an answer to that prayer. Don was ready to once again help his brother with the growing scope of Teen Challenge.

CHAPTER 8

Hope in the Streets

1962-1963

"Evangelism is the heart of Teen Challenge."   — Mike Zello

Don's first ministry assignment upon returning to New York City was to set up a chapel on the boardwalk of Coney Island in Brooklyn. David's street evangelism was growing, and its purpose was to set up booths and chapels in various parts of the city to meet people "on their turf." Coney Island was a tourist site bringing in thousands of people each year, and many of those visiting were attracted to the various booths and rides along the boardwalk.

Don and Cindy moved in with Ann Wilkerson in Staten Island while they established themselves in their new roles at Teen Challenge. Don, Cindy, and Ann (also known affectionately as Mom Wilkerson) made their way each day from Staten Island to 416 in Brooklyn. They would leave their apartment and take a bus to the Staten Island ferry. On the ferry, they would pass the Statue of Liberty on their left and watch the construction of a new bridge called the Verrazano-Narrows on their right. After a twenty-minute ferry ride, they would arrive in Manhattan and take two subway trains before walking several blocks to the Teen Challenge Center. Once they reached the center, they would spend an hour in prayer and have lunch. Next, they prepared with their team and traveled to Coney Island to minister at their booth called the Teen Challenge Surfside Chapel.

The chapel was nothing more than a few collapsible walls with some folding chairs set up each night. They strategically chose a bar as a nearby location so that patrons would have to pass by the chapel on their way to and from the bar. The Surfside Chapel was ironically located across from a popular ride called The Devil's Pit. Each evening during the chapel service, they would sing gospel songs or hymns, have a few people share testimonies about their Christian faith, and pass out literature tracts. To close out the evening service, Don would give a short sermon.

FEAR OF EVANGELISM

Don recalls the night he was to preach his first message at the Surfside Chapel. David knew his brother was nervous about this assignment and agreed to go along to help him get things started. David opened the meeting, and immediately the small crowd was drawn to his message. Don witnessed how at ease David was in front of a crowd. However, Don felt nervous and was out of his comfort zone. He quickly realized that his brother had a natural gift for this kind of work, but he did not. "When Dave called on me to take over the meeting, my knees rattled and my stomach felt as if I swallowed a rock," Don remembers.[49] "Lord, you will have to help me. I can't do it alone." Don struggled with his words, but he eventually managed to take command of the situation. At the end of the meeting, he thanked God for helping him with the ability to preach his first street ministry sermon.

Don and Cindy quickly realized how different their lives were from the previous year in rural Vermont. They went from pastoring a tiny congregation in a quiet community to ministering daily to hundreds of people out on the busy boardwalk of Coney Island. As he continued his street ministry assignment, Don became more aware of his fear of personal evangelism. "As long as I had been allowed to do my preaching and witnessing in a church, I had been in my element. Until I had come to Teen Challenge, my ministry had been pulpit-oriented. For me there was now a fear of stepping out of the pulpit and onto the street corner with the same message," Don shared. "I found that the thoughts I felt I could express in church with some eloquence were now being uttered with labor, if at all, when I faced people on the street."[50]

Like many young ministers stepping into a new ministry role, Don had to trust that God would equip him for this role fully. Neither his pastoral training nor his upbringing gave him the confidence in how to minister out on the streets. Don felt foolish speaking to gang members and drug addicts that he had difficulty identifying with. He was not prepared for the wall of resistance in his attempts to relate to their addiction problems. Addicts would question Don, "Have you ever used drugs?" Don would honestly answer, "No." "Then how can you help me?" the addict would question. Don struggled with these questions and his effectiveness in street ministry.

The only solution Don knew to overcome this fear and doubt was to go to God in prayer. Don knew that if God had called him to this work, then, by the power of prayer, He would help him through it. Eventually, Don gained courage and confidence and became comfortable speaking to people of all ages and backgrounds out on the streets. He found that he was no longer bound by fear and was now guided by the love of God. When others made him feel like an outsider and asked, "How can you identify with me if you have never taken drugs?" Don would answer with boldness, "Does a doctor have to be sick with cancer to help cure someone with cancer?"

GREENWICH VILLAGE

While Don ministered out in Coney Island, Mom Wilkerson would travel down to Greenwich Village in Manhattan. Her outreach encountered the 1960's hippie generation who rejected the idea of God and His existence. While many on the streets were willing to listen and accept the idea of God as hope in their lives, Mom Wilkerson encountered those who argued the existential meaning of life. Her ministry was called The Lost Coin, and it was a storefront, coffee house on Sullivan Street. It was a place where people could casually walk in, pour a cup of coffee, and sit at an open table to carry on conversations. Mom Wilkerson and her friend Faye Mianulli, a Village resident, started The Lost Coin to share the gospel message with those that the city deemed undesirable: teenage runaways, weekend hippies, alcoholics, homosexuals, and transvestites. When residents of Greenwich Village would criticize the coffee house for attracting these "undesirables," Faye would lovingly respond to them, "We don't see them that way."[51]

Mom Wilkerson loved the ministry of Teen Challenge and seemed as if she was born for the role of street evangelism. She found a new calling in life since her husband's death. David took care of her while she supported him and promoted the ministry. She loved to witness on the streets of Greenwich Village, and many called her an apologetic evangelist. She would often gather a crowd near New York University and debate with students presenting proofs of Christianity and why someone needed Christ. It was a sight to see. A petite, older woman debating with intellectual hippies on a street corner. She was bold and never let anyone intimidate her. The late Leonard Ravenhill, who was involved in Teen Challenge in those early days, called her "a cross between a Mother Hubbard and a top police sergeant." She had a combination of boldness and a mother's love, especially when it came to loving people with the love of Christ.

On one particular day, Mom Wilkerson had drawn quite a large group of people around her. A police officer came by and said, "Lady, move on, you're preaching on the street." Normally she would move on, but this particular day she was having a good discussion with two gentlemen and there just happened to be a crowd gathering around the three of them. Mom said to the officers, "Listen, I am talking to these two gentlemen right here and these people (the crowd) are intruding. You get rid of them." Another officer approached Mom, "Lady, if you don't move, I am going to have to call a squad car." She turned to the officer and said, "You go right ahead and bring your paddy wagon here. I could use the publicity!" She was bold like a lion.

Ann would often be asked to teach others how to evangelize on the streets. She always emphasized the importance of prayer. She would tell them, "Pray for people even if their eyes are open." This meant that even if they wouldn't pray with you, pray anyway. Mom Wilkerson understood that when a person prays, you enter into a realm that many people may not understand, but most people had reverence for prayer. Mom would often end a conversation with someone on the street and ask if she could pray for them.

The Lost Coin was a unique outreach for Teen Challenge focused on a different social class of people. Mom Wilkerson described the coffee house, "We permit hippies and others to talk on any subject—

sex, civil rights, Vietnam or politics— but they can only go so far. They are always brought back to the Bible. It's surprising how their hang-ups and questions can be answered from the Bible."

The outreach was established to be a transient ministry. Many of the workers would have only one conversation with a passerby, challenging them to have a personal relationship with Jesus Christ, and never see them again. Some called this a lost cause ministry. Mom Wilkerson would often be questioned, "Don't you think you are wasting your time here with people who don't even believe in God?" Her answer was simply, "We're here!" Ann Wilkerson witnessed seeds planted in people who later came back and thanked her for sharing the message of hope that began a change in their lives. She understood the importance of being present in a community that rejected the gospel and the belief in God. She stated, "Satan worshippers are here. Drug pushers are here. So we need to be here whether they listen or not."

UNDERSTANDING THE BURDEN

Mom Wilkerson's words "we're here" spoke directly to Don's heart. The resistance to the message given often discouraged Don and the team of workers who would go out on the streets, night after night. But encouragement came from remembering that God had called each of them to this work. David's vision for Teen Challenge was never to share the gospel message with song and testimony and then pack up and return to their comfortable church environments outside the city. The vision was to raise up a place to meet the need of the individual and to offer them hope through the saving power of Jesus Christ. Then those that found that hope would, in turn, go out and offer that same hope to others in their community. They were offering Presence Evangelism to engage the world on behalf of Christ.

The more Don went out on the streets ministering, the more he began to identify with his brother's burden.

"I found my heart going out to these people. When I had first come to work among them they frightened me and I hadn't understood them or their way of life. Now I was beginning to comprehend, to see the sociological upheaval that was spewing these people into the streets and sidewalks and gutters. Hundreds of thousands of people shoehorned into this tiny corner of the earth, many of them poorly educated, many of them jobless, many of them bewildered by the world that pressed in on them from all sides. Hope? Fun? Goals? Incentives? Family Life? These people knew none of these things. They existed, rather than lived, which was tragic in itself, but what made it even worse was that they had a hard time finding a reason for existing."[52]

Don learned he needed to have obedience and faithfulness to fulfill God's calling. He was ill-equipped to step into this role. He was a young man in his early twenties with no experience on the streets. He had a very different upbringing than those who he was ministering to. It was interesting how God was using these two brothers on the streets of New York City. Neither of them appeared to fit the role in their physical appearance. Nonetheless, they were obedient to the call, and by God's grace, a ministry was established through them. Don was beginning to feel the burden of those without hope, and God's love ministered through him.

STREET MEETINGS

The Teen Challenge Center was not just a place to rehabilitate gang members and drug addicts. It extended its outreach to help prostitutes, alcoholics, and others with a wide range of problems. Chapels, coffee houses, and street ministries spread throughout the city with the message of hope that Teen Challenge was offering. Perhaps, the most effective outreach ministry for Teen Challenge was its street meetings.

It has often been said that one can never appreciate who David Wilkerson was unless you saw him preaching at an open-air street meeting. During the 1960's, it was quite easy to set up a platform and sound equipment in an area of the city. David and his team would set-up "church" in a crime-ridden area. Groups of workers would walk through the community inviting people to the street meeting. The outdoor meeting would begin with a musical team, and the music drew in curious neighbors from blocks away. Many times the platform would be set-up in the middle of a low-income housing project. People would peer out of their windows from as high as their tenth story apartment building to listen to the sounds below. Then David would approach the platform, and one would immediately understand why God called him to this kind of ministry. He would speak with boldness about the gospel of Jesus Christ in changing lives. His small stature contrasted with his bold voice.

Many of those listening on street corners or park benches had never heard of Jesus Christ. They didn't know about the unconditional love of a Savior who could redeem their brokenness, their addictions, their torn-apart families, or their violence-filled lives. They only knew hopelessness. David spoke boldly, "God is the only one who can cure you! Nothing is impossible with God. If anyone claims cures outside the power of God-they are lying." Reverend Wilkerson did not mince his words. "You must believe that the Bible is the Word of God and that it is true," he would continue. "When you know the truth, the truth will set you free. The Bible makes you this promise: If you confess Him as your Savior-He will make you into a new person. The old life will pass away and everything will become new!"[53]

David would ask those in the crowd who wanted to know Jesus to come forward to the altar. He implored them to lay down their guns, knives, drugs, and alcohol on the makeshift platform. He prayed over them and called them to a new life in Christ. You could feel his burden through his prayer over those hurting and broken in the crowd.

It was the truth in this message and the positive cure of Christ's love and salvation that brought many men and women forward to the platform in tears of desperation. Mothers cried over their drug-addicted sons and daughters. Drug addicts worn out by their constant need for a high placed their drugs on the platform and were ready to be set free. Teenagers who were curious about this message of unconditional love wanted to fill the void of emptiness they felt in their lives.

Many of these addicts had gone through hospitals and treatment centers for their addictions. They knew it didn't work. But, Teen Challenge did not promise hope found in a medical facility or a new drug recovery method. It was simply found in the Bible. That book that

David was asked to hold up in the courtroom in 1958, he held up at the street meetings all across the city. However, now there was a place to offer hope and help restore broken lives.

The Teen Challenge Center at 416 Clinton Avenue was now housing a few addicts who were becoming free from their addictions by this "positive cure." Its doors were open, and evangelism was the root that would continue to grow the ministry. Mike Zello, who witnessed the birth of the ministry, understood the importance of that root. "Evangelism is the heart of Teen Challenge. It was from the very beginning, and it must continue to be, or it is not Teen Challenge," he stated. "There are physical addresses of Teen Challenge programs, but the root of every successful program has and always will be evangelism on the streets and meeting the need of an individual with the saving power of Jesus Christ."

ROOFTOP PRAYER REMINDER

The reality of what God had accomplished through prayer was realized by Don one day when he was tasked to run an errand. Ralph Geigle was one of the first drug addicts to enter the program at 416. One day, David asked Don to drive Ralphie to his apartment so he could pick up some of his clothes. As Don drove into Ralphie's neighborhood, he was directed to the address of South 2nd Street in Williamsburg, Brooklyn. Don looked at the building where Ralphie's apartment was located. He immediately recognized the location. It was the same building where he and David had filmed the rooftop drug scene. Don remembers waiting for Ralphie looking up at the building and a thought crossed his mind. *Could it have been, when we were praying for the Lord to give us an address of hope that Ralphie was in his apartment that day?* No one knew whether Ralphie was there that particular day, but it was another astonishing event from that rooftop prayer. God brought one of the first drug addicts to enter the program from the very same building where that prayer was prayed.

While the government in the early 1960's was struggling to find a way to deal with the growing drug epidemic, and medical institutions were trying to cure those overpowered by drug addiction, a five-story house in the middle of one of the most crime-ridden streets in Brooklyn held the key to addiction freedom. It was the first recognized faith-based rehabilitation program in the country. The message of "we're here" was spreading throughout the city by volunteers and workers who believed that the transforming power of Jesus Christ could change lives and cure drug addiction.

CHAPTER 9

The Jesus Factor

1962-1963

"When I walked through that door, I knew there was something different about this place." —Bobby Lloyd

As the country was battling the growing drug epidemic in the early 1960's, institutions were treating drug addiction through various methods. There was the chemical response of administering blocking agents to stop drug cravings, but at the time this was only used on heroin addicts and proved to be more of a control response than a cure. The sociological method relied on counseling, group therapy, and psychological techniques to confront the addict on their need for drugs. While statistically this method had a higher cure rate than the chemical response, many developed a dependency on the centers where they were treated. Lastly, there was the religious method demonstrated at Teen Challenge. This method was about addressing the spiritual aspect of addiction. One Teen Challenge director concluded about this approach, "There is no denying that evangelical organizations like Teen Challenge, involved in street ministry are achieving remarkable results. But when you bring God into the picture, it is impossible to evaluate these results rationally, and statistics become meaningless."[54] Taking into account each individual's need and letting the Holy Spirit work in each addict's life couldn't be measured with statistical outcomes.

Teen Challenge was proving to be a different kind of method in curing drug addiction.

David and Don had a burden for those plagued by addictions, but they didn't know how to truly cure the addicts. Their spiritual upbringing taught them that the Holy Spirit could supernaturally and immediately change a person from the inside out. On several occasions, they had a street meeting, and a drug user would kneel and pray the prayer of salvation. An addict would be immediately delivered from their addiction through the power of the Holy Spirit. David called this "the thirty-second cure."[55] They would then encourage that recovering addict to go out the next day and evangelize with them. Though there were some instances where God did supernaturally cure an addict overnight, the brothers soon realized it wasn't that simple.

Don remembers that a group of thirty or more workers would go out in the evening to evangelize out on the streets. They would only require one or two staff members to stay behind at the Center to care for those recovering addicts who were "drying out" or withdrawing from the drugs in their bodies. "But we would come home to find only nine left, and the next day eight, and the next day seven," Don recalled. The addicts were unable to endure the withdrawal process adequately. "We came to realize that it was not enough to have them kneel and accept Christ if we were not going to care for them and give them a real chance. In short, we found that evangelism without care and discipleship was not true evangelism,"[56] Don emphasized. They began to understand that addicts needed close supervision with a withdrawal period and 24-hour a day care.

By 1962, the Teen Challenge Center was a residential program for those who needed full-time care and treatment for their addictions. But to be able to establish itself as a positive cure program with proven results, Teen Challenge had to prove this faith-directive approach in rehabilitation. This was a pivotal point for the brothers in fully allowing the Holy Spirit to develop Teen Challenge, letting God meet the need of the individual with a structured residential program.

GOD'S MOUNTAIN

As the brothers allowed the Holy Spirit to teach them how to develop the program properly, all those involved in Teen Challenge witnessed how quickly the Holy Spirit was moving. God was using David's evangelistic talents and his visionary gifts to grow the ministry. David's next plan was to purchase a rural property outside New York City. He witnessed the positive effects of taking former gang members and drug addicts out of the city, out of their life of crime, drugs, and all the temptations that surrounded them in their neighborhoods.

In June of 1962, a Mennonite farmer named Arthur Graybill contacted David and offered to sell his farmhouse with sixteen acres of farmland in Rehrersburg, Pennsylvania. David drove out to see the property and immediately knew this was to be an additional place for Teen Challenge. It was a picturesque farm complete with a white barn, tall silos, and farm fences dividing the land. David envisioned this would be a place where the men in the program could receive training in both spiritual discipleship and skilled labor after leaving 416. On the highest hill of the property, David and Mr. Graybill planted a twig in the ground to symbolize what God would plant there. They prayed over the land and David committed the farm to God. He prayed that it would be a place for former gang members and addicts to be able to grow like a tree in their new faith and be trained as followers of Jesus Christ. Teen Challenge purchased the property, and the next phase of the ministry was established. It was the first Teen Challenge Training Center later nicknamed "God's Mountain" by the first students to go through the training program.

THE MAN FOR THE JOB

As Teen Challenge progressed, David was getting more and more invitations from around the country to talk about the ministry. His book, *The Cross and the Switchblade*, also spread the story about his calling to New York City to work with gangs and drug addicts. While David traveled, Don was in Brooklyn serving in various street evangelism efforts and assisting with the residential program at 416.

"Thousands of people are in need, and if we're going to help them we have to bring these people in," David said to Don. "What we need more than anything is someone who can direct all of our evangelistic efforts and also live right in the Center so he can be on top of all that goes on. I think you're the man for the job, Don."

"I don't know what to say,"[57] Don hesitantly replied.

There David goes again, he thought. It seemed David was always calling Don deeper into the work of Teen Challenge—being asked to live and direct at 416 full-time. This was a more significant responsibility. At only twenty-three-years-old, Don was still finding his way in ministry. It wasn't that he didn't want to accept or wasn't grateful for David's offer, but Don was still struggling with God's call on his life. "In the back of my mind there still flickered a hope that I might be the pastor of a church, an ambition that I might have to forsake for good if I accepted Dave's offer,"[58] Don remembers. Teen Challenge was founded by David's vision, and Don was still conflicted whether or not God wanted him involved as deeply in this work as his brother was.

"There's a whole city out there waiting for you,"[59] David urged.

Don discussed the opportunity with Cindy. This move would be a big commitment for both of them. The positive side would be that they would no longer have to commute to Brooklyn from Staten Island each day. The negative side was that they would not be able to escape from the work at Teen Challenge and would be living in an undesirable neighborhood of Brooklyn. Together they made a decision and committed to living full-time at 416 with those they brought in off the streets.

Don and Cindy settled into their small two-room apartment at 416, living among drug addicts and those who ran with some of the most violent gangs in the city. As a small town girl from Vermont and a preacher's son, their inexperience with gangs and drug addicts was evident. But it was this inexperience that was a testimony that they were truly living by faith. Despite their lack of experience, Don and Cindy were both excited about this new opportunity, and the new residents were becoming part of their family. "Their heartaches became our heartaches,"[60] Don remembers. Both he and Cindy shared the burden of ministering to a community of people broken by sin but redeemed by the hope they found in Christ. It was invigorating to witness those becoming free of their addictions by the work of the Holy Spirit.

DEVELOPING A POSITIVE CURE PROGRAM

Don slowly grew into his new role as Men's Home Supervisor. He knew that there were some definitive methods needed to operate Teen Challenge. Street evangelism was still the root of the ministry. Discipleship was also a key component of the residential program. The primary purpose of Teen Challenge was to administer the positive cure of the gospel or the spiritual component in curing drug addiction.

While Teen Challenge underwent many changes, it was important to structure the program in the most effective way. The goal was to rehabilitate and train those that walked through the doors to be able to walk out entirely free from their addictions and able to be contributing members of society. There were no guidelines or manuals that Teen Challenge could use from other well-established faith-based programs. They were a pioneer ministry, and although they could gather information from secular or medical institutions in treating drug addiction, their spiritual component set them apart in rehabilitation methods. How was Teen Challenge to be structured as a successful program in the day-to-day, hour-by-hour life of the ministry and in the field of drug rehabilitation?

The answer to this question was found in prayer. "The only thing that kept us going and this is as true today as it was then was that we prayed about our needs and could feel God's leading in these matters," Don recalls. "Had we processed on our own, we would surely have done irrevocable harm and probably would have brought Teen Challenge tumbling down around us. With God answering our prayers and interceding for us in so many ways, though, we moved forward."[61]

What evolved through prayer was a three-step program: pre-induction phase, three to four-month induction at 416, and about an eight-month training period at the farm. These three phases came out of trial and error. Each step was given flexibility according to the individual and their progress in the program. The task was to treat the person, and not the problem of addiction. Everyone who walked through the doors of 416 Clinton Avenue had a different background and their own unique story. If Teen Challenge allowed the work of the Holy Spirit to be their guide, then every person would have to be given time to grow in Christ at their own pace to let the Holy Spirit change them from the inside out. There were strict guidelines and discipline used in the program, but flexibility for the individual was a key component to the success of the ministry.

THE INTERVIEW

Perhaps, the most difficult lesson to learn was that not everyone who stepped through the doors of Teen Challenge was serious about becoming rehabilitated. Some took advantage of the help that was offered to them and walked out after time was invested in them. Some stole from the program and left. This meant the first phase- the interview or pre-induction process- was an important part of the program. "It soon became evident that our process of selecting and admitting people would have to be refined," Don remembers. "This was not easily worked out, for judging the sincerity of addicts, we were finding out, was a delicate matter." But admitting those intent on being cured was a crucial part of the success of the program. "One of our earliest strategies, telling an addict who sought admittance that he should come back the next day, was a method that we found to be one of the most reliable tests of how he yearned to get rid of his habit,"[62] Don recalled. However, this guideline was often tested, and Don had to navigate the work of the Holy Spirit through those who walked through the doors.

"You can't let me go back to the streets," Cookie pleaded to Don for help.

"You're high on drugs. I can't let you in here in your condition. Come back tomorrow,"[63] Don told her.

Cookie had been using drugs since the age of fourteen. Now she was a junkie addicted to heroin and financing her drug use through prostitution. Cookie desperately wanted help. The admitting policy was to have her come back the next day, but Don felt the nudging of the Holy Spirit.

Cookie pleaded, "Mister, I want help. Please, you gotta let me stay."[64]

Don gave in to her request going against his own rule. He never regretted his decision. Cookie became clean, accepted Christ, became a wife and mother, and used her life to help others find Christ and become free from their addictions. Cookie's life story changed at the address of Teen Challenge. Don often wondered what would have happened to Cookie if he hadn't been led by the Holy Spirit and allowed her into the program that first day. Cookie was an example of the importance of using flexibility in the program and following the Holy Spirit's guidance in admitting every individual who stepped through those doors. A faith-based center had to be guided by God first and methods second.

THE INDUCTION PHASE

The second part of the program was the Induction Phase. Getting off drugs was not just about withdrawing or kicking the habit; every student would have to learn to live in a community with set guidelines and earn the trust of the staff within the program. Don realized that Teen Challenge had to maintain a tough love approach in dealing with drug addicts. The program made it clear that they did not offer a man-made cure for drug addiction. They provided Christ as the cure, and although they didn't require a commitment to Christ to being in the program, they did require sincerity. "I have often stood in the pulpit in our chapel and told the men and women in our program that we want them either to be sincere about Christ or to leave the Center quietly,"[65] Don said.

This approach might have seemed harsh, but the program's philosophy was based on the belief that a person's behavior can only be permanently rehabilitated by changing their heart. A spiritual self-help method. This was accomplished by applying proven, positive, biblical principles leading to a personal and supernatural conversion experience. Teen Challenge's success in treating addiction stems from the belief that deliverance and freedom can only come through a personal relationship with Jesus Christ. It's a tough love approach, but with the intention of helping a person find peace, freedom, and joy in a changed life.

In the Induction phase of the program, each student was required to join a group of eight to ten residents and abide by the rules of that group. Each team lived together as a family with a staff member. The group would work, eat, worship, and study together. They were purposely mixed racially, educationally, and with different backgrounds to challenge each one to see life from a different perspective.

Many of those who walked into 416 were from broken homes. They never experienced what it was like to live as a family and develop trusting relationships with others. Problems in these family groups were inevitable, but at Teen Challenge each one was forced to deal with these difficulties in the context of how much he needs Jesus. All the walls of sin and brokenness have to come down, but that would take time to allow the Holy Spirit to minister to each student's particular needs.

When Bobby Lloyd entered the Teen Challenge program, he was immediately turned off by the name "Teen" in the name Teen Challenge. He was thirty-eight years old and much older than most of the men in the program. A drug dealer and heroin user, Bobby had already led a hard life of crime out on the streets of New York. His life was spinning out of control by the time he entered Teen Challenge. He recalls his first day walking through the doors of the center, "The name Teen Challenge turned me off, but when I walked through those doors, I knew there was something different about this place."

Bobby's life began to change when he saw things in the students and in the program that he didn't quite understand. He saw one guy with the words "love" and "hate" tattooed on his knuckles, raising his hands and praising God in the chapel. Another guy who came out of the Army had his hands up weeping and worshipping God, as well. "Teen Challenge showed me that there's a higher power than me," Bobby remembers. A drug dealer once accustomed to being in control on the streets with the top drug sellers all over New York City was now witnessing a change in others who were surrendering control and worshipping Jesus.

"There was something about the program that got to the bottom of my heart, and I couldn't escape it," Bobby recalls. "It just doesn't work on the outside of man. The program operates on the inside to change someone who has life-controlling problems. Teen Challenge taught me to put God first." The program was able to reach some of the toughest guys and soften some of the hardest hearts through the love of Christ. Teen Challenge didn't use psychological philosophies, medical interventions, or man-made theories. It simply shared the truth of the gospel of Jesus Christ and used the Bible as a tool to break down the walls of sin that had captured those in a life of crime and addiction.

THE TRAINING PHASE

The last phase of the program was the training period. This was David's vision and the purpose of the farm; to train those who entered the program. Students were only allowed to go to this next phase when both the family group and staff felt they were ready. The training consisted of Bible instruction, academic studies, and vocational training to prepare them for life outside the program. In the end, the hope was that these former addicts would become useful Christians, not only contributing to society but going out and offering the truth they found at Teen Challenge to others.

Raul continually fought the craving for drugs or what he called "the hammer." He had entered Brooklyn Teen Challenge program and developed a personal relationship with Jesus Christ. Raul was a faithful resident who followed his studies and the rules of the program. He had made it to the third phase of the program at the farm in Pennsylvania. He could recite Scripture and declare victory over sin, but the craving for drugs daily plagued his mind. "I couldn't shake the 'hammer'...I was physically clean and sober as far as absence of drugs in my body, but the drug craving-the mind habit-was still present within me,"[66] Raul recalls. How was he going to face the real world with this constant craving for drugs apart from the program?

One day he found deliverance while visiting a church with a group of men from Teen Challenge. "As the pastor and elders prayed, and laid hands on us asking the Lord to keep us and make us strong, I felt the power of God come upon me unlike I'd ever experienced," Raul recalled.

He experienced what many at Teen Challenge called the "therapy of praise," a Holy Spirit experience and a divine encounter with God that produces a complete deliverance. Raul felt a complete change, "When I knelt the next morning for my usual devotions and prayer something was different. The 'hammer' was gone! The mental desire for drugs and a high was no longer in my mind." He waited a little longer wondering if this was truly a reality. "It was still gone. Praise God, I'm totally free! The pressure isn't there anymore," he declared amazed. "Thank you, Lord. I'm free indeed!"[67]

THE THERAPY OF PRAISE

The three-phase program at Teen Challenge made chapel time an essential component of the daily schedule. It was described as the heart of the program where "therapy of praise" was administered. Chapel was when the residents and staff gathered for a time of worship, teaching, and prayer. It's difficult to describe the joyous, emotional worship experience of a room full of recovering addicts. When a resident is delivered from their drug addiction, and their soul craves the healing relationship of Jesus Christ, that healing can powerfully manifest itself. A chapel filled with all nationalities- Italians, Hispanics, African-Americans, Irish- worshipping the God who has restored them is a therapy that is indescribable. A chorus of men and women belting out songs like "Our God Reigns" or "There's Power in the Blood" in both English and Spanish, their arms raised towards heaven, some with gang sign tattoos—the evidence of a former life.

Don would often remind the students that God welcomes all kinds of worship both loud and quiet. "I am convinced that many converted drug addicts think God is deaf," Don exclaimed. "Again and again, I tried to calm down the guys in our chapel services. I even tried to teach them that you don't have to scream at God to be heard! My efforts didn't always work."[68] That chorus of loud praise and prayer was often heard by nearby residents and drifted down the street. Neighbors didn't always appreciate the noise level that came with the students' overzealous worship.

One particular day during chapel time an angry neighbor called the police and demanded that the noise level be addressed at the Center. This wasn't the first time the local police precinct took a call about the noisy activity coming from Teen Challenge. Two officers decided to address the situation and entered the foyer of the chapel area.

"Who's in charge?" the police officer asked.

A group leader stepped forward and replied, "I am, Sir."

"Listen, we appreciate what you're doing, but that noise in there has got to stop. We've had too many complaints. Now go in there and stop that right now," the officer demanded.

The group leader promised that it would be over soon, but the police officer demanded again, that it stop immediately.

"I can't do that," replied the leader. You see, those are all former drug and alcohol abusers in there. They're praying and seeking God. That is their group therapy!"

Without hesitation, the impatient officer opened the chapel door and witnessed a Teen Challenge chapel service filled with former convicts and drug addicts. He saw men crying, praying on their knees, some with hands raised towards God, and an outpouring of the Holy Spirit through prayer and worship. He stood in the doorway taking in the unique scene and quietly backed out closing the door behind him. He turned to the other officer and said, "You go in and stop it."[69] The second officer went in but soon left without giving a warning.

The irony of police officers walking away from a room filled with former drug addicts, many who spent time incarcerated for their crimes, was a testimony to the effectiveness of the Teen Challenge program. The method of "prayer therapy" was unconventional and often criticized as unprofessional in the field of drug rehabilitation. Don explained this unique method, "The truth is what happens in our centers is no more special than what happens anywhere else Christ is exalted, the Holy Spirit revealed, and the Father worshiped in 'Spirit and in truth.' The only difference in our case is that nearly everyone in our 'congregations' is in need of a radical revolution in their lives."[70]

The therapy of prayer encouraged the residents in the program, especially with every individual's needs in recovery. Some of the residents were immediately receptive to the power of prayer. Staff members would be encouraged with a student's progress when they witnessed a recovery addict praying alone at the altar or outside of the regular chapel time. Prayer was a sign of spiritual maturity and a person's willingness to bring their needs to God in overcoming their struggles.

THE TEEN CHALLENGE CORNERSTONE

The most significant difference between Teen Challenge and a federally-funded program is that Teen Challenge puts its hope in the Jesus factor, not in the success of the program. One resident asked Don, "How long is this program?" Don smiled and said, "This program, it lasts the rest of your life." The gentleman looked puzzled, so Don explained further, "I am in this 'program' just like you are! The 'program' is not Teen Challenge- the program is Jesus!"[71]

A person entering the doors of Teen Challenge was seen as more than a physical, emotional, and mental being. They are spiritual beings with spiritual needs. The theme of the program is taken directly from 2 Corinthians 5:17: "Therefore if anyone is in Christ, he is a new creation; the old has gone, the new has come." This Scripture meant that at Teen Challenge addiction was not defined as an incurable disease with a lifetime sentence of possible relapse. From day one in the program, the purpose was more than to become drug-free but to become what the Bible says, "Free Indeed." Men and women were becoming new creations in Christ with a new purpose in life. Teen Challenge was proving, through personal testimonies, that addiction was not only curable but that graduates could be forever changed and embrace a new life.

Bobby Lloyd described the answer to his life transformation at Teen Challenge as simply "Jesus." He testified, "I looked at this man who died on the cross so I could be set free. For me to leave my life dealing drugs on the street and go here, to Teen Challenge, it had to be something unbelievable. And it was Jesus. I needed this man Jesus."

Today, there's a sign in the front hallway of 416. It reads: "Hope lives here. Freedom is found here. Changed lives leave here." This is a message that resonates with many alumni. Men and women walked through those doors broken from their addictions and walked out restored with hope in their lives. They could now testify to a positive cure for their addictions. It wasn't a man-made cure. It was the cure found in Jesus Christ—the cornerstone of Teen Challenge's success.

CHAPTER 10

The Power of Prayer

1964-1966

"Prayer saved my career at Teen Challenge."

—Don Wilkerson

The 1964 World's Fair in New York City featured a Teen Challenge exhibit with its break-through solution in tackling the national drug problem. The ministry was gaining recognition as a successful drug recovery program. David would often tell the staff members, "If we really meet human need, the world will beat a path to our door." Teen Challenge was meeting the human need by helping people find freedom from drug addiction. Street meetings were now including testimonies of men and women who were cured of their addictions. Drug addicts from Harlem would listen to a testimony of a former neighborhood junkie who was now free from addiction and practically unrecognizable because of their physical transformation. That beaten path to the door of Teen Challenge was paved by every graduate who would go out and testify that they found a cure through the hope found in Jesus Christ.

The ironic part of the growing success of Teen Challenge was just six years before, David walked along the streets of New York City and had no idea what a drug addict was or how to help one. Now God had established a three-phase program in the heart of New York City. God was using both David and Don despite their lack of knowledge about drug addiction and recovery. They were ill-equipped and—at times— naïve, but they had a burden to reach those bound by life-controlling problems. The brothers acted in obedience and, as a result, God was using their obedience to build a successful faith-based program. One former drug addict described the brother's burden as simply "genuine." He noted, "It's very hard fooling a street person and a drug addict. If you are genuine, we'll know it. There was something genuine about both brothers."

Perhaps, even more, ironic is that God used these two brothers— raised under the strict guidelines of their Pentecostal upbringing—to start a ministry that abounded in the grace of God to the individual. Both David and Don grew up with an overemphasis on rules or a works theology. However, they were also exposed to the importance of discipleship and the understanding of the Scriptures under the pastoral ministry of their parents. And they were nurtured in a caring family home of security with their siblings. All of this helped to develop Teen Challenge as a rehabilitation home. In the end, their upbringing, which would seem to oppose what the brothers created, was what shaped the ministry. They balanced a strict discipline approach with the beautiful work of the Holy Spirit to disciple and soften a heart towards finding freedom in Christ. This balance of rules and grace was not always easy in structuring a home for addicts. In fact, it was one of the challenges in the very name of Teen Challenge. But the lives of these brothers and all their experiences were coming full circle for the glory of God.

SAVED BY PRAYER

David continued to travel promoting the ministry of Teen Challenge. Churches of all denominations, groups, and individuals wanted to learn more about the courageous minister they read about in *The Cross and the Switchblade*. David was also getting invitations from radio and television stations, and various publications were writing about his ministry. David Wilkerson and Teen Challenge were becoming well-known names in many Christian circles throughout the country.

With David away for weeks at a time, responsibilities fell on Don to manage the Center. He reluctantly became the de facto director of the program. Supervising a home of recovering drug addicts was a 24-hour-a-day job. Don's previous assignment as an Outreach Community Worker allowed him to go home at the end of the day. Now the Center was his home. Don found that whenever there was a crisis—whether it was two o'clock in the morning or two o'clock in the afternoon—he was responsible. It wasn't long before he experienced the pressure of this new position and the everyday challenges of running the program.

Teen Challenge was growing and was now able to offer hope to not only men but women. They purchased a new building across the street from 416 and started a Teen Challenge Women's Center at 405 Clinton Avenue. When there was a need for expansion, they would pray, and God answered that prayer by adding new addresses to the ministry. But with every new phase of the program came more paperwork, more residents to supervise, more workers, and more costs. Just as quickly as David would raise funds, more funds would be needed. It seemed as if Teen Challenge was constantly understaffed, overcrowded and underfunded.

Don remembers the stress, "Finances at Teen Challenge were so low that there were many days when we weren't sure where we would get the money to pay for the next meal for all the people at the Center. When we did have food, it was often poorly prepared. We were badly understaffed, our men's dormitory was overcrowded, and we were unable to find anyone who could cope with the female addicts."[72] This financial struggle was all too familiar. It was just several years ago that Don, David, and their mother Ann were depending on the day-by-day funds to establish Teen Challenge. Now, the program needed financial resources for a larger number of both students and staff.

One day, while David was at the center during meal time, the dining room area was particularly overcrowded. Each table was filled with residents and staff. Benches lined the walls for additional seating. Some men were eating their meals along the steps of the staircase balancing their trays on their laps. Don approached his brother. "Just look at that," he pointed to the men along the staircase. "We can't go on like this." David calmly turned to Don and said, "I'm as aware of the problem as you are. The Lord knows about our problem, too. I've been up late at night in prayer."[73]

Don respected his brother's tenacious prayer life. He witnessed all the changes at Teen Challenge and in David's own life that directly resulted from his willingness to pray. But Don was feeling resentful over the burden of dealing with the day-to-day struggles of the program while David was off traveling. David didn't have to lie awake at night worrying if there would be enough food to feed the residents. He didn't have to watch a drug addict leave the program and wonder what he could have done differently to get him to stay. David also didn't know the toll this was having on Don and Cindy's marriage. The nights Don would spend in the office way past dinner because of the demands of his work kept him from spending time with Cindy. "My focus became fixed on Dave," Don remembers. "Dave doesn't have to travel that much," Don would think. "He's out there having a good time, and I'm back here doing the work that belongs to him."[74] Don began to put all the blame on David, and this put a strain on their relationship.

Young age was also a source of Don's stress. Supervising the program in his early twenties meant that he was almost half the age of some of the men who entered the program. Before, Don would never have thought of this as an issue, considering his dad had instilled in him to "never let anyone disregard youth in ministry." But not everyone viewed age in the same way his dad had.

Don approached an older resident of the program one day to find out how things were going for him. "How are you doing?" Don asked.

"Not so good," the man replied.

"What's the problem?" Don questioned.

"I'm having a problem taking orders from you. You are just a kid," the man bitterly responded.

Don smiled and said, "Actually I'm older than you. In this place, we don't just look at biological age but spiritual age. I am much older than you in spiritual years, and this qualifies me to help you." Don was referring to the fact that the man had not yet committed his life over to Christ and he was struggling in the program. The man nodded his head in agreement and said, "Pastor, you got me there." Nevertheless, Don felt the sting of this resentment about his young age and had to overcome this challenge with many older residents of the program.

Despite Don's struggles in leading the ministry, there were days that Don felt the work was rewarding. "There were always converts around the Center, people who had been rehabilitated and were now free of drugs," Don remembers. "They were an encouragement to all of us [the staff]."[75] Don would feel revitalized about the work, but then—with each passing day that his brother was away—he would feel the anxiety, and it would take a toll on his health and his marriage all over again.

Don's naturally thin six-foot frame became even thinner. He wasn't eating or sleeping properly. His mom, Ann, realized that Don could not handle the burdens of this new position. "Maybe this is not the work God wants you to be in?" Mom Wilkerson questioned. "Don't you think you'd better go back to pastoring?"[76] Don appreciated his mother's wisdom and counsel. She could relate her struggles of pastoring with their father Kenneth and was an uplifting voice to both her sons. She was also constantly concerned about the different personalities of the brothers and how those different traits could lead to a potential falling out between them. Don wondered if his mother's advice was right. Then one particularly stressful day, Don decided that was it. He would quit. *Obviously*, he thought, "God did not want me at Teen Challenge any longer."[77]

Don began to list in his mind all the reasons why quitting was the right decision for him. "My health was being ruined, my married life was being constantly intruded upon by the demands of the work, and my outlook in general had reached an all-time low," he listed. "Gone was the glamour of the work. Also missing now was the fervor with which I had approached my duties in days past. Clearly, something had to be done,"[78] Don concluded. Now he had to decide how to resign and break the news to his brother. He decided to write a well-thought-out resignation letter to David. Don would explain his reasons for leaving and also rehearse a bold speech to follow the letter. He would wait till his brother returned from a recent trip and would inform him of his resignation.

While Don waited for David to return, he began to feel more and more uneasy with his decision to resign. "In what seemed to me to be a strange turn of emotions, I sensed that I had no feeling of relief about quitting,"[79] Don remembers. He couldn't shake this uneasiness in what should have been a peaceful decision based on God's leading. He knew there was only one way to find out what was happening in his life. "I went to the bedroom, closed the door and began praying," Don recalls. "That next hour or so may well have been the most important of my life, resulting as it did in a new and fuller relationship with the Lord."

Those hours spent in prayer revealed to Don the number one reason that the past year had been so full of stress, anxiety, and one struggle after another; he wasn't praying. Don tried to accomplish too much on his own and forgot that there was abundant strength through prayer in which he could lean on. He started to question how he could have forgotten to put prayer first. After all, Don witnessed the evidence of prayer first hand in David's journey to New York City to minister to the boys who were on trial. The 416 building was a direct answer to the brothers' prayer offered on that rooftop after filming heroin addicts. Don's mother and father also had demonstrated the importance of prayer in their pastoral ministry. He grew up with the spiritual wisdom of his father's words, "God always makes a way for a praying man." He knew this, but somehow he had lost his way.

That vital prayer conversation entirely changed Don's outlook. "Prayer saved my career at Teen Challenge,"[80] Don exclaimed. "What God did for me during those hours of prayer was simply to give me a good lesson in anatomy," Don recalled. "He shook me by my heels, extracted my foot from my complaining mouth, set my eyes upon Him, opened my ears to reality, pointed my nose straight ahead and reminded me that my progress would be swifter if I would get down on my knees more often in prayer."[81] Don realized he was trying to do things in his own strength and it wasn't working. "I was getting in my own way so much that I had become my own worst enemy," Don remembers. "When I took time to pray and to be honest with God, He made it clear that we would tackle the job at the Center together." Don could rest on the understanding that his job included bringing the many needs of Teen Challenge to God in prayer and waiting for Him to answer. Don now understood why his brother could look at the overcrowded room at meal time and assuredly say, "God knows about our problem." David let prayer be his first response in times of uncertainty. Prayer was his security.

God used prayer to spiritually mature Don for his leadership role at Teen Challenge. He thought about his days in the mailing room doing the menial tasks and eagerly helping David launch the ministry. Back then, God had taught him the importance of being a faithful servant in the little things. Now, Don understood that as a leader assigned to more responsibilities, he had to be committed to lead in times of stress and financial pressures 24-hours a day.

What wasn't evident at the time was that God was working behind the scenes to develop David and Don's gifts, personalities, and skills purposefully for the future of Teen Challenge. David was a visionary leader with ambition. He always anticipated the next step for Teen Challenge. David had a prophetic voice as a minister of the Gospel. His God-given ability to preach to large crowds and evangelize brought people to Jesus Christ. But, unlike David, Don identified the immediate needs of the program. He was able to minister one-on-one with those in the program. God was developing Don's pastoral gifts purposefully for rehab work with men and women who walked through the doors of Teen Challenge. One resident described Brother Don, as they called him, as a practical leader, "He looked at situations and told it like it was. But he told it in a way that brought healing and not harm. Brother Don made you look at your problems and laugh at them and then give them to Jesus."

Don's breakthrough prayer time gave him a renewed purpose at Teen Challenge and a new respect for his brother. He knew God was uniquely using David's evangelistic skills to tell of the work of Teen Challenge. But he also realized that his yearning for a pastoral position was already a reality. No, it wasn't a typical church setting, but Don acted as a pastor and a spiritual father for those in the program. One particular verse encouraged Don. It was Paul's warning to the Corinthian Church, "Even though you have ten thousand guardians in Christ, you do not have many fathers..." (1 Cor. 4:15) God was calling

Don not just to be a pastor but a father to the recovering addicts of the program. This was a leadership role that the Holy Spirit had been preparing him for since he was a teenager, and specifically for this particular time at Teen Challenge. The brothers were working together for the future of the ministry despite being separated by travel and circumstances. "We seemed to work together, yet apart because we understood each other's gifts," Don recalled. "I knew I could not do what David did in ministry and he saw the same in me. Our differences were an asset and not a liability." One staff member described the brothers' partnership, "David had the vision and insight, but he depended on Don to carry it out and fulfill it."

Don's renewed calling to put prayer first also helped him to understand how to be a role model to the recovering addicts in the program. When he had taken every burden and problem of the Center upon himself to solve, it taught the men and women of the program to rely on him for answers instead of leaning on God. Don now realized that prayer was the most effective tool in helping an addict because it taught them to turn to God for their needs and struggles.

AN EFFECTIVE TOOL

One month in 1964 was particularly difficult for Teen Challenge financially. The need for funds was substantial, and—if money didn't come in within a week—Teen Challenge might have to close its doors. David gathered the residents and staff in the chapel, and he led them in prayer over their monetary situation. It was a Thursday, and David prayed that they would receive funds by Tuesday of the next week. For five days, the students and workers lifted this need before God in prayer. On Tuesday, a check came in the mail for 10,000 dollars from a woman in Pittsburgh, a large sum of money from a woman who had no idea of the financial crisis at Teen Challenge. God had answered their prayer. They passed the check around, and some women were crying so hard that David warned, "Don't get the check wet." Don remembers the joy on the faces of the people around the Center when they heard the good news. "Some fell on their knees and thanked God, others raised their eyes heavenward and shouted out a prayer, and some, overcome with joy, sat down and wept."

The financial burden of running this type of rehabilitation ministry was a testament of the Jesus factor in the program. Prayer was the focus. There was an expression at Teen Challenge that said, "We live from hand to mouth—from God's hand to our mouth."[82] Government assistance did not financially support the Center. The program depended solely on contributions from people who believed in the work of Teen Challenge. Both Don and David realized that the power of prayer was the reason for the ministry's success. It was also effective as a lesson to the new converts on how to depend on God. Don was once asked why Teen Challenge went through such difficult periods of financial stress. He answered, "I think one of the reasons is that it is the Lord's way of showing us that He still answers prayers. Another reason is that the dramatic answers to our needs have helped to strengthen the faith of Christians everywhere, especially in our program."[83]

PRAYER, FAITH, AND GROWTH

The next need brought before God in prayer was to expand the program to a larger facility. Both the buildings at 416 and 405 Clinton Avenue were overcrowded. The brothers discussed plans to purchase property outside the city to house the residents. They would keep 416 as the main office building and as a place to interview addicts for admission into the Center. Don was excited about the opportunity to build a brand new facility that would meet the needs of the expanding program. He was also eager for the opportunity to move Cindy and their new addition to their family, their daughter Kristy, into the suburbs.

The brothers looked at real estate in both Staten Island and Long Island. Every time a property came on the market and bids were put through for purchase, plans would somehow fall through. One particular estate in Long Island seemed to be the answer for their new facility. Unfortunately, the people of the town decided to meet together and organize an effort to halt the purchase. They did not want to bring those "kinds of people" into their neighborhood. Teen Challenge was not welcome. Don remembers the struggle with the communities, "If a town didn't have a law we would have violated by moving in, then everybody scurried around and wrote up a law lickety-split that would take care of us. Instant laws were our undoing." Don reflected, "I couldn't help wondering how those people would have felt toward us if they or one of their loved ones had been in our program trying to kick the drug habit."[84]

The fact was Teen Challenge was welcoming people into their recovery program that others considered the "undesirables" of a neighborhood. Besides drug addicts, there were former prostitutes, drug dealers, convicted felons, alcoholics, manic-depressives, and a variety of people of all nationalities and cultures. These people were seen as outcasts and not deemed appropriate for small-town America. The reality was people did not want a recovery program like Teen Challenge in their community.

Don became discouraged over the difficulty in finding a new property. Then the brothers started to pray, and both felt that maybe the reason there was so much resistance was that the program was supposed to remain in Brooklyn. One day David, Don, and their treasurer walked down the block and looked at the buildings along Clinton Avenue. David approached the owner of 436 Clinton Avenue about purchasing the building. He introduced himself, and the owner said, "I know you; you're with the drug addicts." David replied, "Yes, and I'd like to buy this house!" The owner laughed and said, "Reverend, you may be doing a good work, but I've been remodeling this place. We have thirteen apartments here." David told the gentlemen that he had been praying that God would give him this building. The man firmly responded, "No, we're not selling. Besides, you couldn't afford the price; I'd want $90,000."[85] David gave the man his business card and said he would continue to pray.

Two days later the owner of 436 called and decided to sell the property. The family had suddenly decided that they wanted to move to the suburbs. It didn't matter to David that Teen Challenge didn't have the 90,000 dollars to purchase the building. He prayed, and God opened the door. Complete confidence was often David's mode of operation. He somehow always had the faith to pursue a project despite the lack of funds. Sometimes he would make decisions, ignoring the requirement of the Teen Challenge Board to vote on a matter. "He saw things through the eyes of faith," Don recalls, "It was as the Scripture says, '...certain of what we do not see.' (Heb. 11:1) It was seen through

THE POWER OF PRAYER

David's eyes, and he did not tolerate a lack of faith in others if he felt God was speaking to him."

David then looked at the property next to 436 and knocked on the door at 444. He offered to buy the property with the vision to tear down the building and build a brand new facility. There was even an additional lot to purchase behind 444. Each time David approached the owners, but the properties were not for sale. David said he would pray and within days the owners decided to sell. It was evident that God had provided the answer to their prayers. They would expand Teen Challenge along Clinton Avenue.

The real test of faith was that all three properties required a large sum of money that they did not have in their bank account. If Teen Challenge were to remain in Brooklyn, then God would have to provide the financial means supernaturally. Everyone at Teen Challenge began to pray. They all interceded for provision: office staff, counselors, residents, Mom Wilkerson, Don and David's families. Then the miracle happened. "Within three weeks God had supplied the money so that we were able to pay off all our debts on our new properties in cash," Don remarked with amazement. "All of us bowed our heads in prayer. There were many tear-stained faces and many happy faces, but all were bathed in the utmost sincerity of a people who had witnessed a miracle."[86] It was divine intervention, and God was fulfilling His purpose for Teen Challenge.

In 1966 Don was officially appointed as the Director of Teen Challenge. David would oversee the program in its entirety as the Executive Director while continuing to travel. Plans were drawn up to build a brand new facility on the lot at 444, and, after months of planning and construction, a new building was dedicated in prayer in July 1967. The men of the program lived at 416, staff lived at 436, and the office headquarters was now located at 444. The women's Center at 405 Clinton Avenue eventually moved to Garrison, New York. A wealthy businessman named Walter Hoving helped purchase a beautiful twenty-three-acre property outside the city for the women's program. The land included a Tudor style home large enough to provide housing for all the women. The directors, John and Elsie Benton, renamed the property as "The Walter Hoving Home" in honor of Mr. Hoving's generosity.

The newly constructed Teen Challenge headquarters at 444 had a 1960's modernist design style, vividly painted with white and blue bricks. It prominently stood out among the run-down brick tenements along Clinton Avenue. There was even a lawn area at the entrance of the building—a rare green space in a ghetto environment. The new facility included offices, classrooms, a chapel, a large dining room and kitchen, and enough space for the expanding ministry. On the front of the building were the words "Teen Challenge Center" marked with bold black lettering against the white brick. It was not merely a name on a building, but a testament to the power of prayer.

Don looked out of the window of his new office onto the green lawn and reflected on his ministry role at Teen Challenge. He began to think of all the people who had beaten a path to the doors of the program seeking help: the rich and the poor, the prostitutes, the drug-pushers, the strung-out addicts, the sick and the lonely. Men and women from all nationalities and various backgrounds were overcoming their life-controlling problems in choosing to follow Jesus Christ. Each new address of Teen Challenge was meeting human need by offering freedom from drug addiction.

CHAPTER 11

The God Professionals

1966-1968

"Prayer was our one tool, and if we didn't use that tool- we had nothing."
　　　　　　　　　　　　　　　　　　　　　　　　—Pat Larson

Teen Challenge grew because of prayer and faith. Both David and Don realized that, for God to continue to sustain the ministry, it had to not only be Christ-centered but prayer-focused. Don reflected, "No one had done before what we were doing. And no one but the Holy Spirit could show us what to do. We had to pray and ask the Holy Spirit to teach and lead us."

Because it was a faith-based ministry, Teen Challenge had to recruit staff that had Biblical knowledge. They also needed young people to help build the ministry. This is why David often spoke at Bible Colleges all over the country and extended an invitation to come to Brooklyn and work at Teen Challenge. He captivated young students with this exciting new ministry on the streets of New York City. Many of these students had already read *The Cross and the Switchblade* or heard the miraculous testimony of Nicky Cruz and his conversion from gang leader to Christ follower.

JOHN AND CAROL KENZY

Unknowingly, the burden to help drug addicts in New York City was already being birthed in the hearts of young people by the Holy Spirit. John Kenzy first heard about Teen Challenge as a teenager while reading a youth magazine. There was an article about Nicky Cruz and how Reverend Wilkerson ministered to Nicky and the gangs of New York. John felt the Lord urging him, and he told his youth pastor, "I am going to go to New York."

When John was a freshman at Central Bible College in Springfield, Missouri he heard about a summer team from school being sent to Brooklyn to work at Teen Challenge. John immediately felt compelled to go, but he didn't want to go purely out of an emotional response. He knew that if he were to go to New York City, it would have to be because God was purposefully calling him to work there. John was from Nebraska and to be motivated to travel all the way to New York City from his small-town life, it would have to be a divine calling. He decided not to join the team.

That summer between his freshmen and sophomore year, John worked on a farm. He recalls his lunchtime prayer sessions, "On my lunch break I would take my brown paper bag and sit by a tree near the farm fields and pray. But I rarely ate my lunch because my prayer time focused on my burden for the people in New York City. Sometimes, I didn't even open my lunch. In fact, tears would be all over the brown paper bag." John felt such an overwhelming call from God to go to New York City and work at Teen Challenge. He was determined if they sent another team that following summer, he would go. David Wilkerson traveled back to Central Bible College to speak with an invitation for a team to come and work at Teen Challenge. However, this time they could only accept twelve people. John applied but told them, "Whether you accept me or not, I am coming to New York City to work." John was emphatic about his decision. He didn't want to experience another regretful summer working on the farm when he knew God wanted him to go to Brooklyn. His greatest desire was to share the gospel of Jesus Christ on the streets of New York City—a desire that he knew was God's purpose for his life. Fortunately for

John, he was one of the twelve chosen to work that summer at Teen Challenge.

John was just one of the many people that the Holy Spirit guided to work at Teen Challenge. The brothers' burden to reach those plagued by drug addiction was shared by many who would walk through the program's doors. God was using the most unlikely candidates to help those with life-controlling problems. Many were from Middle America and grew up in small towns. They did not know about drug addiction and had no knowledge of city life, but what they did have was the motivation to share the love of Jesus Christ. Don shared, "We were truly living out the familiar quote that 'God doesn't call people who are qualified, but calls people who are willing and then qualifies them.'" This became a repetitive calling—birthed in the hearts of others—for the future of Teen Challenge.

After interning at Teen Challenge for two summers, John graduated from Bible College and was hired full-time along with his wife, Carol. They were a young, newly married couple working alongside David and Don Wilkerson and the various staff at Teen Challenge. John had previously helped Don at the Surfside Chapel in Coney Island, as well as developing the first Biblical curriculum for the program. He was now teaching the students and working with leadership as the Director of Education. Carol worked in the office as a secretary. She too had a God-inspired calling to New York City.

Like John, Carol was also from the state of Nebraska. She remembers a specific movie that she watched in high school about drug addicts. "I didn't even know what a drug addict was at that time," she recalled. "I remember the last scene of the movie showed a man walking in between two tall buildings in New York City and the narrator said, 'There is no hope for a drug addict.'" Carol thought to herself, "Of course there's hope for a drug addict because Jesus can do anything." That year of high school was 1958, the same year David Wilkerson was called to New York City. Carol commented, "God had planted a seed in my heart. I had no idea that my future would be working with my husband with drug addicts in New York City at Teen Challenge."

Looking back, it was as if God was planting seeds for the future harvest of Teen Challenge workers. While David and Don were busy with the demands of this new organization, the Holy Spirit was directly tugging on the hearts of people all over the country—people who were drawn to the ministry to serve in many different capacities. There were times when David and Don would pray for a specific position to be filled in their staff, and God would miraculously bring someone in to fill it. Don recalls the many people who were prayed in, "We believe that through prayer, the Holy Spirit is the best recruiting agency we could have. It does not cost us anything except prayer."

RANDY AND PAT LARSON

Randy Larson was from North Dakota. He was attending Bible School when he was invited to do his last year's internship at Teen Challenge. He had read *The Cross and the Switchblade* and heard Nicky Cruz's compelling testimony. He wanted to be used by God in ministry, so at twenty-one years old, he set out for New York City arriving by his first plane ride on October 1st, 1966 at John F. Kennedy airport. He was overwhelmed by the airport's size and the number of terminals. He realized he was a long way from his one-terminal airport in North Dakota.

Outside the airport, Randy waited for someone from Teen Challenge to pick him up. Two men drove up, a staff member named Al and Benny a recent Teen Challenge graduate. Benny was saved from drug addiction and a life of crime off the streets of New York. Randy recalls looking at Benny sitting in the front seat. "I distinctly remember sitting there and seeing Benny. He looked like he had just gotten out of prison and wanted to kill me." Despite Benny's life transformation, he still had a tough New Yorker street persona. Randy had grown up in how he described it as a "monoculture" atmosphere. New York City was his first real experience with different cultures and nationalities. Randy admitted, "Moving to Brooklyn was different from anything I ever experienced in my life."

When Randy first walked into Teen Challenge, he was surprised that there were no teenagers there. He took the name literally, not knowing the diverse age group that was now in the program. Randy soon became accustomed to ministering at the Center and was characterized as always working with a smile on his face. Don recalls Randy's early days at the Center, "He was a hard worker with a servant's heart. Randy was willing to do anything that was needed from fixing a car, running errands, or helping with students' needs. He could lead worship and was able to wear many different hats in the various roles he took on." After Randy's internship was over, he decided to stay on as a staff member working full-time at the men's Center. He eventually met, fell in love with, and married a young secretary at Teen Challenge named Pat.

Pat was raised on a farm in Tennessee. She first heard about Teen Challenge while living and working in Memphis with her sister. When Pat was seventeen years old, she had a near-fatal lung disease. Over time she was cured, but that near-death experience led her to the decision that she wanted to serve God in ministry. Pat prayed and asked God to lead her to a ministry position. Her sister had attended a large gathering at a Memphis Assemblies of God Church. David Wilkerson was the special speaker, and he shared about the ministry of Teen Challenge. He said to the audience, "We need workers." Pat's sister came home and told her all about the ministry, David Wilkerson, and how they needed staff members. Pat recalls, "I kept hearing those words in my head, 'We need workers.' They haunted me, so I decided to write a letter to Teen Challenge." Don eventually answered Pat's letter and said, "Come to Brooklyn."

In February of 1967, Pat traveled many hours on a Greyhound bus to Penn Station, New York City. When she got off the bus, she realized that she had left her purse on the seat. Pat asked the driver if she could get back on the bus to find her bag. The purse was gone, and she eventually found it in a trash can. Her wallet was empty of the cash except for one quarter. She used that quarter on a pay phone to call someone at Teen Challenge. It was her first experience in the big city of New York, and it was frightening, but Pat saw the hand of God in it. "It was as if God left that one quarter so I could make a phone call," Pat remembered. "I felt that was such a sweet thing the Lord did for me." She made the phone call, and Al answered and told her to just get on a subway. Pat answered in her thick southern accent, "I don't even know what a subway is!" She was eventually picked up by a staff member and arrived at Teen Challenge ready for this brand new experience in ministry.

Pat remembers the excitement of living and working at Teen Challenge and witnessing lives changed. She worked in the office and wasn't directly involved with the students of the program, but she remembers the testimonies. "It was always amazing to go into the chapel and see the difference in people," Pat recalled. "Lives were changed, and we became good friends with the people in the program and even after they graduated. The ministry was what we were called to do, and everything we did was to win people to the Lord and eradicate drug addiction."

Randy and Pat Larson were more examples of those who came from all over the country to help and work at Teen Challenge. Many were unfamiliar with life in large urban areas like New York City. They had no experience in drug addiction rehabilitation, but they were willing to be used by God. Don would often receive criticism of the program's lack of trained professionals in the field of drug addiction. It was true that Teen Challenge did not employ doctors or psychiatrists trained in drug recovery methods. "Our rebuttal is that we have found that hours of prayer have been much more beneficial to our patients than hours of psychiatric treatment," Don admitted. "We know that whatever success we have had at Teen Challenge has come through the power of God. Hospitals and other centers for treating addicts have failed to recognize the single most important dimension of the people they are dealing with—their spiritual lives."[87]

Randy was often asked how he could work with drug addicts when he never used drugs or was an alcoholic. "It was always the issue of love for me," Randy stated. "Love for God and love for the people who walked through that door. It's not any more complicated than that." Pat added, "In our minds, we were the professionals. We were the God professionals. Every day was so exciting to see what God was going to do because something great was always happening in the lives of the students in the program. Prayer was our one tool, and if we didn't use that tool-we had nothing."

COURAGE AND GOD'S CALL

Teen Challenge has never opposed professional Christian counseling methods. But Don often warned about the potential to lean more toward the professional side of recovery than the spiritual. "We are determined to never turn our program over to those who depend more on counseling techniques than the power of God through the work of the Holy Spirit,"[90] Don proclaimed. Any doubts or criticisms assailed on Teen Challenge were refuted by the demonstration of graduates who walked out in freedom from their addictions. One graduate described the program as, "a place where you find the answer—the cure—to the struggles of life. You still have struggles, but you now know the God of all comfort."

Those who worked at Teen Challenge quickly realized it wasn't a glamorous ministry role. In fact, the Center was often understaffed which meant they had to put in many long hours assisting the students with the many demands of the program. It was a 24-hour job with very little pay. The city was also a cultural shock for those who traveled from the mid-west or other rural areas of the country. Teen Challenge was located in a dangerous part of the city. There were gang territories, drug corners, and crime all over the streets. Carol Kenzy remembers the shock of living and working in Brooklyn, "The cultural shock was difficult. It was obvious I didn't fit in. I had to be chaperoned on my way to the subway. It was dangerous. But I was never afraid because I knew we were supposed to be in New York City and God would take care of us."

David would often encourage the workers with the Scripture in 1 Corinthians 1:27: "But God chose the foolish things of the world to shame the wise; God chose the weak things of the world to shame the strong." He used the example of David, the shepherd boy, going against Goliath. Those that worked at Teen Challenge were battling the giant known as drug addiction. It was new territory in the work of faith-based drug recovery. There was no way they could achieve success at Teen Challenge in delivering people from drug addiction but through the power of Jesus Christ. Don reflected on all those that God brought to work and minister at Teen Challenge, "We didn't necessarily see ourselves as God professionals as much as we knew that God was working through us. I can't emphasize enough the thing that gave us the strength to face the never before challenges of combating drug addiction. It was the overwhelming sense of God's call on our lives."

CHAPTER 12

Beyond 416

"Give the ministry away."   —David Wilkerson

During the summer of 1968, Teen Challenge celebrated its 10th Anniversary. David and Don and their Board of Trustees, staff, students, and families were all gathered outside of the new building at 444 Clinton Avenue. It was an exciting day for the ministry. They were celebrating all that God had done in just a decade. Not only had they created a home for those lost and addicted to drugs but numerous buildings lined the streets of Clinton Avenue with the name Teen Challenge on them. The ministry was growing and expanding so fast. It was difficult to keep up with the growth: The Teen Challenge Center in Brooklyn; the Training Center (Farm) in Rehrersburg, Pennsylvania; the Walter Hoving Home in Garrison, New York; the Greenwich Village Coffeehouse; crusades; street meetings; outreaches; and the most recent phase of the ministry—a training school.

David Wilkerson and the story of *The Cross and the Switchblade* had gained notoriety in the country. It wasn't just the book itself but what it represented. Churches and Christian communities of all denominations were drawn to this David and Goliath type story. A small town pastor reaches out to the outcasts of society and brings a cure to drug addiction. It was a modern-day story of a transformed life, and it was groundbreaking for the Church at that time. The Church did not know how to reach the lost and addicted. Culturally, at the time, people moved away from those broken in addiction and crime. The Church was in a sort of spiritual bubble. The Teen Challenge story opened the eyes of the Church and forced them to see the needs of the people that these brothers were ministering to.

Many would travel to New York City to see the program. They wanted to understand how it worked and how to evangelize. It wasn't long before Teen Challenge centers started to spread into other states. Chicago, San Francisco, Boston, Philadelphia, Los Angeles and Detroit were just some of the cities where Teen Challenge programs were extending. This growth led David to make the decision to allow the Assemblies of God to become the headquarters for the Teen Challenge ministry. He understood the importance of accountability with all the programs opening up around the country.

The best part of this growth was that many of the staff members, in all the various centers, were graduates of the Brooklyn Teen Challenge program. Men and women cured of their addictions wanted to help establish other Teen Challenge programs across the country. This was a natural process that developed over time with future Teen Challenge leaders coming out of the program.

Nicky Cruz had gone on to Bible School, worked in Teen Challenge, and then became a minister and evangelist. He was a natural born leader. Before Christ, his influence was on the streets, but after receiving Christ, Nicky used his leadership skills for the gospel. It was the indigenous principle similar to missionary work. Missionaries would bring the good news of the gospel to people in third world countries and then train people to continue to reach their own community. Similarly, in Teen Challenge those reached were in the ghetto and drug subculture. Don Wilkerson called this the "fourth world." Both David and Don understood that the best people to reach those in the "fourth world" were those who had been saved from it.

A TRAINING SCHOOL

David realized that the men and women who wanted to go and work in Teen Challenge Centers needed education and discipleship. At first they sent graduates to well-established Bible Schools throughout the country. However, they soon realized that many of those who came out of the rehab program were not a good fit for mainline colleges. One reason was that these former Teen Challenge students were often a novelty in these schools. The popularity of David Wilkerson and the Teen Challenge ministry put them on a pedestal. Many of the students could not handle the pressure and intrigue placed upon them. Another reason was that many of the graduates of the program were not academically ready. They needed schooling that was tailored to their specific needs academically, culturally, and spiritually. Teen Challenge was a unique rehabilitation program that required a special school for the students to prepare them for life beyond the program. So David's next vision for the ministry would be a school to train Teen Challenge graduates to become leaders.

David approached John Kenzy, the Director of Education, with his idea of a training school. They had found a property in Rhinebeck, New York, and David asked John, "Would you prayerfully consider going to Rhinebeck to set up the school to train pastors, evangelists, and missionaries?" This question was timely for John. He was praying for direction in his life. He knew he was supposed to continue to work in Teen Challenge. After all, that was the burden God placed on his heart since he was a teenager, but he was feeling called out of the city. "I kept praying for direction," John remembers. "I felt God was calling me out of Brooklyn, but he wasn't taking the burden for the people out of me." John shared his concerns with David. Putting his hand on John's shoulder, David said, "John, God always makes a way for a praying man." John prayerfully made the decision to leave Brooklyn and go and direct the school.

The Teen Challenge Institute of Missions (TCIM) was described in a letter by David Wilkerson as the "miracle school." He wrote, "We had no money but we had a big God. We asked Him to perform a miracle and make it possible for us to obtain the property for a training institute.

God did provide the necessary funds! A unique Bible training center is now functioning and today the miracle is still unfolding."[91]

Once again, David's prayerful vision for the next phase of Teen Challenge was realized by faith. It was a school to train former drug addicts and other Teen Challenge graduates to become men and women of God who would go back into drug neighborhoods and work for Teen Challenge centers in the United States and overseas. The school eventually transitioned to admitting anyone who wanted biblical training. Gail Dill entered as an eighteen-year-old. She never had a drug background, but her brother went through Teen Challenge, and she witnessed his life transformation through the program. She attended the school because she wanted to work in the Teen Challenge ministry. It was a unique school with people of different backgrounds and of all ages with an educational program tailored to each student.

The school eventually relocated to Sunbury, Pennsylvania. It was renamed Youth Challenge International Bible Institute (YCIBI). John and Carol Kenzy have been in leadership of the school since its founding. John has served as President of the school for over fifty years. The Kenzys are examples of two people who were given the burden of Teen Challenge and used that burden to lead people further along in the ministry. The school trained future leaders for Teen Challenge. This was a vital component of the faith-based rehabilitation method of drug recovery. "The Kenzys taught us to live by faith and trust God for the next step in our lives," said Floyd Miles, a TC graduate. "It was a humble school, but produced so many men and women of God to share Christ around the world."

A HOLISTIC DRUG RECOVERY PROGRAM

As director, Don began to understand the importance of this phase of the ministry. "For years I believed that once a Teen Challenge student completed the residential program, our responsibility was over. We'd give them a Completion or Graduation Certificate and bid them Godspeed to the next phase of their life. How wrong I was to think that our responsibility ended after the residency phase of our program, especially when I saw many fall back into their former lifestyles."[89]

Teen Challenge was naturally developing into a holistic drug recovery program. David's philosophy from day one was that in Jesus Christ there is a total cure for the total person. This meant that after graduating and recovering from addiction, a person would develop their new life in Christ. For any given graduate, this meant a job in a drug recovery program like Teen Challenge, ministry, business, parenting, or whatever God was calling someone to in their new life in Christ.

Ten years of this natural progression from evangelizing on the streets of New York, to an addiction recovery program, to a training institute was the reason why Teen Challenge became a successful ministry. "I would often be asked by various people how we decided to start all the different phases of a rehab program from a farm to a school," Don commented. "In this type of ministry, one thing leads to another if you let it." The key component of Teen Challenge was that evangelism led to this natural process. Don further stated, "Our motto became deliverance, discipleship, and destiny. We are here to help you! We are here to deliver you! We are here to disciple you! And we are here to help you find your destiny!"

Teen Challenge was using a biblical pattern in drug rehabilitation, and it was working. People were finding freedom from their addictions because the spiritual component of recovery was vital to a person's transformation. The address of hope at Teen Challenge was producing other addresses of hope, and the world was taking notice.

GOD'S PLAN

There was also another natural process taking place in the ministry that many didn't realize, especially Don Wilkerson. By 1970, David had decided to step away from Teen Challenge to minister full-time in his David Wilkerson Youth Crusades. He moved his family out to California as a home base from where he would travel full-time around the world. His youth crusades were packed full of teenagers and young adults in large arenas. David had the gift of evangelizing youth and warning them of the dangers of drugs. These weren't gangs or teenagers from the ghettos. They were middle-class kids, many from church upbringings. They were drawn to David's story of his journey to New York. David and Don's sister, Ruth, writes, "David was labeled an alarmist because he told parents and church leaders that their children were being seduced into a life of bondage to drugs, alcohol, and lawlessness. Few parents, ministers, or school officials believed these young people would be the next generation to be addicted to drugs."

God had called David into a whole new realm of ministry as a full-time evangelist. It was a timely transition as this was amidst the Jesus Movement of the late 1960's and 1970's, a period where huge revivals were taking place mostly along the west coast among hippies and the generation from the 1967 Summer of Love in San Francisco; a generation popularized by sex, drugs, and rock and roll. God was using David's story for a different generation lost in addiction, the same burden but to a new social class of people.

Meanwhile, Don was back in Brooklyn, and the Teen Challenge ministry was now under his leadership. It was a natural transition for Don, but many people didn't know that David was officially gone from the program and Don liked it that way. "I was an untitled leader for years at Teen Challenge," Don recalled. "I came from a generation where we didn't need titles. I was a servant of the Lord. Teen Challenge was founded on David's vision and his leadership alone. But what naturally evolved under me was a team ministry dependent on numerous people." Teen Challenge was now empowering graduates and other people to carry on the work, and Don was facilitating this process. Don was uniquely gifted for this role in rehab work, but it took him a while to understand this as God's unique plan all along.

One day this realization of God's plan for Don came from his brother. David had returned to Teen Challenge to visit with a pastor friend. He was giving the man a tour of the program. David introduced the pastor to Don and said, "This is my brother. He does all the work, and I get all the credit." Don felt encouraged by David's public recognition. "It was the first time I realized that David understood my ministry role and that was important to me," Don admitted. Don's ministry skills were suited for rehab work and were purposeful for Teen Challenge. "David had encouraged me in my abilities, and I had to, in turn, do the same for those working in ministry with me. I had to remember to give credit where credit was due."

Teen Challenge was never meant to be a David or Don Wilkerson ministry. That was never God's intention; and, had it stayed that way, it probably would not continue to exist. But God had a plan. He used one brother's act of obedience to the streets of New York City to be the founder, and another brother's gifting to adopt that vision to be the father of Teen Challenge, a vision now carried on by countless servant leaders around the world.

A Teen Challenge graduate described the brothers, "Pastor David needed someone he could trust to take on the mantle, and his brother Don was that person. David knew that Don was faithful and would fulfill the vision and purpose that God had given him for Teen Challenge. David went out and planted seeds, but Don watered and developed those seeds, and there was growth even out into the world. God needed these two brothers."

Don remembers David teaching him something very valuable early on in the ministry. David said to me, "Give the ministry away," Don emphasized. "Let God use other people in their own way. It is why we have supported other similar ministries of our graduates. Many are doing the same type of faith-based drug rehab work but under a different name. David was never married to the name Teen Challenge, and he taught me to not make an idol out of this ministry."

Those who have the advantage of looking back over the past sixty years understand that God specifically ordained these two brothers to impart the mission of Teen Challenge. One graduate described the legacy of the brothers, "The Wilkerson legacy is to bring forth hope and it is simply about Christ. That's a legacy to have and that legacy is now being passed through me."

Over time the ministry has adapted to meet the needs of those they serve. Today the ministry is called *Adult and Teen Challenge* to reflect the diverse ages in the program. It's natural for any organization to adapt and change through the years, but the DNA of the founding is still the same. It's not a complicated mission. It's simply the gospel message. It was founded on a heart's calling to reach the lost and the broken. Teen Challenge was never meant to be only about drug rehabilitation. It was and continues to be about the message of redemption and a personal faith creating life rehabilitation through Christ.

CHAPTER 13

Legacy

INTRODUCTION TO TEEN CHALLENGE TESTIMONIES

As I was writing this book, I had the honor of attending a memorial service for a man named Pete Rios. Pete graduated Teen Challenge in 1969. He was a former heroin addict from Brooklyn, New York. Pete attended the Teen Challenge Institute of Missions (TCIM) and became a leader in the program while I was growing up in the ministry. I grew up with Pete's kids. I had my first taste of Spanish rice and beans in their home. We were staff kids who played together and we thought we owned the place. We were a big deal!

It was a privilege for me to sit there at Pete's memorial service, a man I knew from my childhood days and to support and comfort his family. I listened to his family members, my father, and Teen Challenge graduates talk about Pete's life. Pete Rios was an example of the total cure of the total man. He took his rehabilitation and shared it with others in their recovery. Pete left a lasting legacy. As people began to share about Pete and the impact he had on their lives, it all of the sudden hit me. This powerful feeling of sheer humility came over me. This man's life was a part of the legacy of Teen Challenge and my family was a part of his life transformation.

I recently read a quote about family legacy. It read, "At its simplest, I've been given a stunning heritage I did nothing to earn; and that's the beauty of legacy. It's the gift we leave for others."[92]

Teen Challenge is a legacy of people; my family, those who have served in the ministry, those who have found hope through it, and future generations of families restored— breaking the cycle of addiction. And I was given the privilege of being born into this legacy, a gift that I now fully appreciate and will always cherish.

So this chapter shares a few stories of the Teen Challenge legacy from the past sixty years. They are testimonies of people's lives that found hope through the ministry but they point to a bigger story—a spiritual story. At Teen Challenge, it is never too late for God's redemption. The gospel is legacy!

REDEMPTION FOR A SUICIDAL ADDICT
Mariah Noelle Freeman / Walter Hoving Home (2010)

Many people can accurately describe their childhood as a happy time in their lives. Mariah Noelle Freeman is no exception. She has wonderful memories enjoying life as an active kid who loved sports and dancing. Mariah's family was active in their local church, and she enjoyed all the activities related to church life. There was a glimmer of light and happiness in her childhood years with a bright future. But at the age of twelve years, circumstances changed drastically for Mariah. Her family pulled away from their church and "God wasn't a part of our family life anymore," Mariah recalls.

It was during those adolescent years that a shadow fell on young Mariah's joyful, innocent childhood. "It was like a light switch went off in my life, and I started to hate who I was," Mariah remembers. By thirteen years old, Mariah started to act out her self-hatred by cutting herself and through bulimia. She was often bullied in school and was desperate to feel liked and accepted. Anger and thoughts of ending her life consumed her. Doctors put her on Prozac because of her mental instability. She was admitted in and out of psych wards. Mariah reached for anything that would numb the pain: marijuana, alcohol, cigarettes. She even began to snort Ritalin and Adderall that she would purchase from friends.

By the age of sixteen, Mariah tried cocaine for the first time. "As soon as I tried it, I knew it was all over for me," Mariah remembers. This new addiction led her down an even darker path. The cocaine just reinforced her self-hatred, and thoughts of suicide constantly plagued her mind.

Then at seventeen-years-old Mariah found out she was pregnant. She began questioning everything at that point. How could she raise a child? Would she graduate from high school? What about the health of the baby? She was an addict taking many different drugs. Mariah became consumed with guilt and everyone that surrounded her told her that abortion was the right choice for her. "My eyes were blinded to reality and what the truth was," Mariah reflected. "I didn't understand or know what love was or who God was. I was so blinded and confused."

Mariah was scheduled for an abortion at Planned Parenthood at three months pregnant. She remembers feeling like the whole procedure was an out of body experience. "I felt the frigid temperature in the room and the cold manner of the people who surrounded me. They used terminology I didn't understand. They said things like procedure and fetus. No one mentioned the word baby," remembers Mariah. "Everyone treated my situation and my scheduled abortion as a normal thing, but I felt so removed from reality."

Starting cocaine at sixteen years old was a downhill spiral, but after her abortion, Mariah completely checked out of life. "My abortion was like a fast slide down to hell. You don't think you can go farther than cocaine addiction," Mariah remarked. "But you can go a lot farther than that." After barely graduating from high school, Mariah began to prostitute herself out for drugs. Her life spun completely out of control. Her parents kicked her out of the house, and she would move from place to place carrying plastic garbage bags with a few of her clothes and possessions. She was arrested twice for driving under the influence and found herself checking in and out of various psychiatric hospitals. Thoughts of suicide continued, and she felt hopeless. "I was more of a suicidal addict than a drug addict," Mariah admitted. "Drugs were like a weapon to get me to end my life. I was driven to be done with it all more than I was driven to get high. I overdosed numerous times, and I should have died, but God had other plans for my life."

One day, Mariah was waiting for a guy to purchase her so afterward she could go and buy drugs. He took one look at her and said, "I am not paying for this!" It was in that humiliation that she realized she couldn't go on. "That was my moment," she reflects. "I couldn't even prostitute myself. I knew I was sick and needed help." Mariah had a pamphlet that a friend had given to her about a program called the Walter Hoving Home. She had placed it in one of her plastic bags of clothes and for some reason never threw it away. She called the program, and they told her she needed to come off every drug before they could admit her. Mariah was overwhelmed with the prospect of having to come off every drug. She was on a dozen prescription medications, a high dose of Methadone, still shooting heroin and cocaine into her arms, smoking crack cocaine, and smoking cigarettes. She had to come off everything completely. Mariah's psychiatrist cautiously asked her, "Are you seriously going to do this?" Mariah knew what this meant. She understood how difficult it would be for her body to come off every drug, but she was determined.

Ready for help, Mariah's parents allowed her back into their home where she went through 3-months of medical detox. It was torture. Mariah felt unbelievable pain, sleepless nights, and was hallucinating as her body was withdrawing from the drugs. At one point in the detox, Mariah remembers sitting in the bathtub and crying out, "God, if you are real, please, help me through this!" It was at that desperate moment that Mariah felt God's immeasurable grace. Mariah testified, "It wasn't me who was able to go through that and get off all those drugs. It was God holding my hand and helping me. I was so desperate to get free from drugs, and I could feel God's grace—grace upon grace upon grace—through it all."

When Mariah was physically able to make the six hour trip to the Walter Hoving Home, she admitted herself into the one-year rehabilitation program. She was twenty-four years old and was committed to finding the freedom she so critically needed in her life. It was a continuous struggle, and her cravings for drugs were so strong. She suffered from a constant migraine and sleepless nights where she could only sleep about 2 to 3 hours at a time. The drugs had taken a physical toll on her body, and she had to endure post-withdrawal symptoms. Mariah found strength in understanding who Jesus Christ was in her life. "Every time I continued to seek God in my struggle, he would answer me and give me comfort," she testified. Mariah witnessed many other women in the program graduate walking out in freedom. She saw hope and joy in their lives and Mariah wanted that in her life. She was so tired of living in darkness and pain.

The Walter Hoving Home was a place of refuge for Mariah. She began to read the Bible, pray and seek after the things of God. She held on to the Scripture in Hebrews 11:6 that says, "...He rewards those who earnestly seek him." Mariah remarked, "I was so thirsty for the things of God and was seeking Him for everything. I began to experience the Holy Spirit, and He began to reward me with understanding the questions of my life. I felt this unexplainable peace." It was at the 9th month of the program that she finally was able to sleep through the night. She had a full seven hours of restful sleep. She had not experienced sleep like that for years. Mariah stated with joy, "I remember it like it was yesterday. I woke up completely refreshed and renewed. It was such a gift from God." There was healing both inwardly and outwardly from her addiction.

Mariah graduated from the program with a new purpose for her life. It was a long year that she calls a "treacherous journey" to find freedom from not only her drug addictions but her suicidal thoughts as well. "Each day God was giving me enough to sustain me. I found hope and grace every day as I continued to heal," Mariah remembers. God had transformed Mariah's life. She was a living example of Ezekiel 36:26, "I will give you a new heart and put a new spirit in you; I will remove from you your heart of stone and give you a heart of flesh."

That first day of graduation she traveled to Brooklyn, New York City and enrolled at Brooklyn Teen Challenge's School of Ministry, a one-year leadership and ministry training program. That led her to work as Don Wilkerson's assistant, as well as gave her the opportunity to travel and do missionary work in four countries in Africa. Mariah is the author of *From Heroin to Heaven* where she shares her journey of triumph over addiction. She feels called to help other women find freedom from their addictions. She regularly visits a local jail to talk to women about the love of Jesus and her testimony of deliverance.

Today Mariah lives out her freedom from addiction married to a godly man, and they have two beautiful children. Her example of God's grace is how abortion spiraled Mariah into one of the darkest times of her life to now blessing her with the precious gift of motherhood. She now radiates the light of Christ into her family so her children can experience the joy of a happy home and childhood.

Mariah has no doubt that had she not walked through the doors of the Walter Hoving Home she would either be dead or institutionalized.

She not only found the salvation of Jesus Christ, but she found a family of life-long friends. When asked about the legacy of Teen Challenge that led to the creation of many women's rehabilitation programs like the Walter Hoving Home, Mariah remarked, "The legacy is family. That's what it was founded upon, and that is what it continues to be." A family environment that many graduates travel back to and remember their place of healing and restoration. A home where for even a suicidal addict like Mariah, God proves nothing is too hard for Him to redeem.

◇◇

HARLEM, THE REVOLVING DOOR, AND BREAKING FREE

Floyd Miles III / Brooklyn Teen Challenge (1982)
Floyd and Mary Miles / Youth Challenge International Bible Institute (1985)

Breaking the cycle of addiction in a family can be one of the most difficult obstacles to overcome with drug addiction. Floyd and Mary Miles have dedicated their lives, through the ministry of Teen Challenge, to help men and women break free from drugs to restore hope to families. Both of them are living examples of this hope.

As a young man growing up in the ghetto of Harlem, New York City, Floyd had a revelation about his future that would change the direction of his life. At the time, he was at his lowest point, living in an abandoned building strung out on cocaine and the hallucinogenic drug known as Angel Dust. "I believe God showed me that life in my neighborhood was like a revolving door," Floyd remembered. "I saw young people like me and the old-timers and realized if I did not get help that the cycle of addiction would continue. I would just replace the older people, and I would never get out of the revolving door. I saw my future, and it did not look good."

Floyd's drug use was coming full circle from his family. When he was just six years old, his mother died from a heroin overdose. His earliest memories were feeling the incredible loss of his mother. "I remember as a child sitting in the living room and repeatedly bumping my head against the chair for hours crying, 'Mommy, Mommy... I want my Mommy'," he said. His father was also a heroin addict. He recalls his dad peering through the fence while Floyd played outside at recess during school. "If I saw him looking at me, he would run away," Floyd recalled. "He did this because he was a hardcore heroin addict, the kind of addict you rarely see today. He was beaten down with abscesses all over his body and would nod in and out of consciousness." Floyd lived full time with his grandmother. She endured the grief of the deaths of her two daughters taken by alcohol and heroin addiction. Drugs eventually seduced Floyd, and his grandmother prayed for his salvation. Floyd remembers hearing the prayers of his grandmother, "Lord, whatever it takes to save my grandson. Don't let him go to hell!"

It was Floyd's father who made the first move out of that revolving door of addiction. "One day, while I was hanging out on the stoop with my friends, I saw this well-dressed man approach me carrying a Bible. It was my dad," Floyd remembered. "He took me upstairs and told my grandmother and me that he had gotten saved through a ministry called Teen Challenge in Brooklyn. God had delivered him from nineteen years of heroin addiction in an instant." Floyd's dad was one of the miraculous testimonies in the early days of Teen Challenge where men and women were instantaneously cured of addiction.

Floyd had no interest in being a Christian like his father. He was happy for his dad and that he found a cure but Teen Challenge wasn't for him. "I felt that my dad needed Teen Challenge because he was a hardcore heroin addict. My drug use didn't go that far," Floyd regrettably admitted. It wasn't long before Floyd's life spiraled out of control where, at the age of twenty-three, he was living in an abandoned building because of his drug use. Floyd acknowledged, "I was at the lowest point of my life, and I remembered my dad telling me for years about Jesus and Teen Challenge. It all started to make sense. It was then that I cried out to God, reached out to my dad, and entered Teen Challenge in 1981."

Within ten months, Floyd graduated from the Teen Challenge program—drug-free—and was ready to return home to his grandmother. "Instead of going home, I decided that I would strive to make something of myself and have a place where my grandmother could live with me if she wanted to," said Floyd. He planned to join the Air Force but instead felt God calling him into the ministry. He entered Youth Challenge International Bible Institute (YCIBI) in Sunbury, Pennsylvania where he met his future wife, Mary.

Mary's life could have gone in another direction if it weren't for God intervening in her family. Her mother was a graduate of New Life for Girls, a drug rehabilitation program founded by Brooklyn Teen Challenge graduate Cookie Rodriguez. After graduating the program, Mary's mother attended the Bible Institute in Sunbury. Mary spent her teen years hanging around the school and was friends with both students and staff. "If I was rebellious, the only place I could go if I was grounded was the Bible School," Mary recalls. Mary's mother prayed that Mary would not rebel into a life of drugs but would follow Christ. "God kept putting people in my path, speaking life into me, and reminding me to love Jesus," Mary acknowledged. In 1982, at eighteen years old, Mary accepted Jesus Christ into her heart. She attended YCIBI, and in 1985 married Floyd Miles.

YCIBI was a school that directed Floyd and Mary to pursue the call of God in bringing hope to people battling addictions. "My faith was made sure at that Bible School," Mary reminisced. "It was such a unique school because some students came from a background of drug addiction and some grew up in the church. But we all had a calling into ministry." Mary served on the prison team while at school and had the opportunity to share the gospel with a family relative that was serving time there. "It was also the same prison where my mother had served time, but it was because of Teen Challenge and YCIBI that my family was transformed. That could have been me incarcerated in that prison, but instead I was sharing the hope of Jesus Christ there," Mary testified.

Floyd continued his education after YCIBI receiving both an undergraduate degree and a master's at Seminary. Together, Floyd and Mary pioneered the first men and women's Teen Challenge program in Connecticut. Floyd is an ordained Assemblies of God minister and has previously pastored in Connecticut and Indiana. Today, the Miles live in San Antonio, Texas where Floyd is the Executive Director of the Adult and Teen Challenge Men's Program and the Director of Operations of seven centers in Texas. They have four children and three grandchildren.

Floyd rejoices in his life that was not defined by that revolving door of addiction. He and Mary are living examples of the Scripture in Jeremiah 29:11: "For I know the plans I have for you, declares the Lord, plans to prosper you and not harm you, plans to give you a hope and a future." Both their families found hope through ministries of Teen Challenge, and the cycle of addiction was broken. The hope found at Teen Challenge not only restores individuals but families and future generations. In addition to his dad, Floyd's sister and his first cousin also graduated from Teen Challenge. Floyd also gives praise that God answered his grandmother's prayer. She lived to see her grandson saved from drug addiction living out the hope of Jesus Christ.

The Miles family have ministered for over half of the sixty years that Teen Challenge has been in existence. When asked the main component that makes the ministry successful, Floyd answers, "We have kept the main thing the main thing! The basis of the ministry is love. It is not rocket science. Teen Challenge loves people through their mess. They loved me through my mess. Teen Challenge shares the power of the Holy Spirit to deliver an addict. The program demonstrates love, and it is that simple."

Floyd continues to live out God's calling on his life. He shares, "I plan to continue to serve in the wonderful ministry of Teen Challenge with my beautiful wife. Together we will use our gifts to serve Him as best we can and to make loving each other, our families, and those we minister to a priority." When the cycle of addiction is broken in a family, God miraculously transforms lives for His purposes.

THE BEST-KEPT SECRET
Greg Dill / New Orleans Teen Challenge (1977)
Greg and Gail Dill / Youth Challenge International Bible Institute (1981)

Greg Dill grew up in Louisiana in a middle class, two-story brick home with a loving mother and father. The family was raised in the Baptist church attending both Sunday and midweek services. He was a kid that had no excuse to rebel, but at thirteen years old Greg took his first sip of alcohol and was hooked by addiction.

His alcohol use led to marijuana, pills, and "dropping acid" or what was known as the hallucinogenic drug LSD. By fifteen years old, Greg was intravenously using drugs and had his first criminal arrest. At the age of sixteen, Greg was arrested in an armed robbery and sentenced to a mental hospital for drug rehabilitation and diagnosed as an alcoholic. "I was medically diagnosed at sixteen years, but I had become an alcoholic a year earlier at fifteen," Greg admitted. His addiction got worse with barbiturates, opioids, and then intravenously injecting alcohol into his veins. "I was so warped that I figured you don't get drunk until the alcohol gets into your blood system," Greg recalls. "Why go into the stomach lining when you can go straight to the blood?"

At the age of twenty, Greg was arrested for the third time. On the bottom of his criminal record, someone described him as a "possible career criminal." In his prison cell, Greg called out to God in prayer. "I prayed my 'if' prayer," said Greg. "Lord, if you are real and if you can change my life, I want to be different." The Judge sentenced Greg to work for his restitution and mandated that he receive outpatient drug rehabilitation.

Greg wanted to attend the residential New Orleans Teen Challenge program, but because of his mandated work sentence, he had to receive outpatient rehabilitation. The parole officer allowed Greg to attend a weekly Bible Study at Teen Challenge for a year, and this counted as Greg's rehab. "It was a miracle in itself," Greg testified. "Statistically, staying clean as an outpatient and living in the same neighborhood where I hung out and did drugs, should not have worked. But God saw my heart and knew I had to obey the courts. By the grace of God, I became drug-free and haven't looked back for forty years."

After completing his work sentence and graduating from New Orleans Teen Challenge, Greg decided to attend Youth Challenge International Bible Institute (YCIBI) in Pennsylvania. It was there that he met a young eighteen-year-old girl named Gail. At fifteen years old, Gail knew she wanted to work in a ministry like Teen Challenge. She had witnessed a transformation in her older brother who graduated drug-free from the Philadelphia Teen Challenge program. Her family was greatly influenced by the change in her brother as well as those they met in the program. Gail wanted to work for a non-profit ministry where she could help make a difference in people's lives. "I knew a Bible degree from a liberal college didn't make sense for me. I needed to attend a school to train me to work in a ministry like Teen Challenge," Gail stated.

Both Greg and Gail graduated from YCIBI fully equipped with skills to serve in a Teen Challenge ministry. "The school trained us to know the Word of God and how to apply it to someone through ministry and counseling. The teachers and staff prepared us for every facet of ministry from the menial tasks to leadership roles," noted Gail. The Dills graduated in 1981 and were married in the chapel on the school grounds. They traveled to Folsom, Louisiana where they began to work for the Teen Challenge ministry there. Today, nearly thirty-seven years later, the Dills now serve as Executive Directors of Teen Challenge centers across the state of Louisiana, including New Orleans Teen Challenge where Greg found freedom from his drug addiction. "We didn't leave YCIBI intending to be Teen Challenge directors, but as years went on, God has used us," stated Gail.

In 2005, the Dills ministry was significantly tested during the tragic circumstances from Hurricane Katrina. Their building on Franklin Avenue in New Orleans flooded under six and a half feet of water. "Before Katrina, we were a struggling day-to-day program like most ministries, but after Katrina, we lost our building and nearly 99% of our supporters," Gail recalled. Most of the financial support for New Orleans Teen Challenge was from local businesses who were also flooded and financially ruined by the hurricane. "It was devastating! All we could do was pray," the Dills remembered.

God answered the Dills prayer beyond their expectations. They had lost a half a million dollars in the property but in just 18 months donations came pouring in, and they were able to rebuild the center without sending requests for funds. "We received donations from other Teen Challenge Centers and individuals around the country. It encouraged us because we realized we were not alone. It taught us to receive from others, but also to be more generous with our own ministry," Gail testified.

Since Hurricane Katrina, Louisiana Teen Challenge has grown exponentially. They have eight programs across the state and were able to open a home where women could be with their children while getting the help they need for their addictions. "Some babies have been born in our facility, all because of the grace of God adding to our vision for the ministry," said Gail.

The Dills have witnessed individuals and families fully transformed through the ministry of Teen Challenge. "I am a testimony that change is possible," declared Greg. "I could have gotten life without parole, but because of Christ, my life changed. Teen Challenge is a place of change, refuge, and peace."

Greg and Gail were called by God to minister to people through the ministry of Teen Challenge. They have witnessed the legacy of this ministry that is life-changing. "Nothing about Teen Challenge is man-made. It's supernatural! It should not have happened, but God called a man named David Wilkerson to New York City with a sincere burden for a sincere change in the lives of others. Teen Challenge is one of the best-kept secrets!" Greg emphasized.

The Dills are beautiful examples of why the ministry of Teen Challenge has continued for sixty years. God takes a former drug addicted convict and a young girl with a passion for making a difference in people's lives and calls them to work at Teen Challenge, leaders who continue to stay true to the same sincere calling of why Teen Challenge was founded. The secret of this ministry is that while the country still battles drug addiction, Teen Challenge leaders and workers like Greg and Gail Dill are humbly offering the transforming cure of Jesus Christ that is life-changing. It's a sustaining faith-based cure without recognition. They simply have a burden for the people in their state of Louisiana. Greg states in his thick southern drawl, "We wear the Teen Challenge badge proudly!"

FROM GANGSTER LIFE TO VICTORY
Frank Livoti / Long Island Teen Challenge (1997)

It's no exaggeration to start Frank Livoti's testimony by characterizing it as a story straight out of a mob movie. Goodfellas, The Godfather, and even the Sopranos television series come to mind as Frank shares about his life growing up as an Italian American in Brooklyn, New York City.

Frank was born in 1967 to immigrant parents from Sicily. They lived in the predominately Italian neighborhood of Bensonhurst, often called the "Little Italy" of Brooklyn. He described his community as the minor leagues of organized crime. Frank remembers at a young age wanting to be a gangster. He watched many of his peers recruited into mob life in his neighborhood.

In his teen years, Frank started smoking and dealing marijuana. He also began to project a reputation where you didn't want to mess with Frank in the neighborhood. He worked both as an elevator mechanic and as a bookie. "I was loaning out money and wasn't learning much about the elevator business. They should have fired me but because of my reputation I could basically do whatever I wanted," Frank admitted. He was not a very big guy in stature, but his reputation on the streets preceded him.

By the age of nineteen, Frank found out his girlfriend was pregnant, and they had a shotgun wedding at the insistence of the father-in-law. By twenty-three, Frank and his wife had three small children. They both tried to make the marriage work. They attended church and Frank attempted to stay clean and sober for his family. "We were babies having babies," Frank acknowledged. "I was very immature, and we weren't properly mentored." The stress and demands of raising a family at such a young age started to take a toll on Frank. "A friend of mine asked me if I wanted to get high on cocaine," Frank remembers. "I thought a little cocaine might make me feel better. But that one high lit a fuse in me that would last for nine years of addiction."

His cocaine use led to smoking crack cocaine, which was the popular drug of the late 1980's and early 1990's. Frank's life began to spin out of control. He spent less time with his family, and his marriage began to fall apart. The drugs made him paranoid, and he described himself as a raging maniac. Meanwhile, his neighborhood was in turmoil as well. His friends were overdosing on drugs, and some were murdered in the streets. Frank remembers, "One of my friends was thrown off a seventeen-story building for robbing drug dealers. I witnessed him dead on the ground. This was my neighborhood. As Italians, we didn't talk about any of these things because it was just reality."

A near overdose experience led to Frank's first attempt to get clean off drugs. It was also a time in his life where he was searching for God. "I always had something in me for the things of God, but I didn't know what it was. I knew about God at a young age, but I didn't know how to have a relationship with him," he acknowledged. Frank entered a 45-day program where he got clean and sober. He was ready to get back to his family and start fresh. When he returned home to Brooklyn, he found his wife had moved out with the kids. "It was all her fault," Frank sarcastically noted. "Of course, nothing was my fault, and before I knew it, I was back on drugs."

Once again, Frank found himself controlled by his addiction. Then he found out his wife was dating another guy. The boyfriend was an Italian gangster in the private sanitation business. Frank was angry and wanted revenge. He often got into fist fights on the streets with the boyfriend. Eventually, the Italians in the neighborhood called for a sit-down. "This is what gangster bosses would do when there was a dispute in the community amongst Italians," Frank explained. "Instead of killing each other, we would settle it in a sit-down." Each guy (Frank and his wife's boyfriend) had a representative from the mob family. Frank's brother was also at the meeting. They all sat down trying to settle this dispute with respect. "They told us to get along and said we were Italians and we need to all stick together," he recalled. "They made us shake hands."

Frank started to find a sense of peace that this dispute might have resolved itself, but then his representative pulled him and his brother aside after the meeting and said, "I want you to bury that guy!" When an Italian gangster says "bury" it doesn't mean to kill but to hurt someone enough to put him in the hospital. Frank had reservations about this, but he also knew that if an Italian boss tells him to do something, then he better do it.

Several months go by, and Frank continues in his addiction, living back in his mother's house strung out on cocaine. He then realizes he needs to get help. He decides to get clean and plans to enter Long Island, Teen Challenge. Frank starts to detox off the drugs, goes back to church, and gets things ready before beginning the year-long program. Then his brother approaches him in the grocery store and says, "We got him (his wife's boyfriend). He's in in the barbershop getting a haircut. Let's jump him now!" Frank starts to question how he is going to do this. He is trying to get clean and is about to go into a drug rehabilitation program. "I am not proud of what I did," Frank admits. "But when Italian gangsters say something has to be done then you don't question it."

Frank and his brother enter the barbershop. It was the same place where John Gotti—the head of the Gambino family—would often get a haircut. They found the boyfriend leaning back in a chair getting a shave. Frank's brother hands him a baseball bat to let Frank take a swing at him. "We walk in, and the first thing I do is grab one of the small hand mirrors and hit him over the head with it," Frank remembers. "I figured if I hit him on the head with the mirror it would be a lot better than to hit him with a bat. Plus I wanted to take a swing at him before my brother did. I was worried my brother would kill him."

The place ignited in an uproar. Both Frank and his brother were trying to hurt the guy while others began to stand in the way to defend him. The boyfriend ran out the door, and Frank's brother puts a fifty-dollar bill on the counter and apologizes to the owner. "You are not supposed to mess with someone's business in the neighborhood. So my brother and I jump this guy but then we end up paying for his shave and haircut," Frank recalls in laughter.

Both Frank and his brother walk to a payphone to put the fight on record. "We call my representative, and we tell him we got the guy in Sal's Barber Shop," said Frank. "We tell him that we messed him up pretty bad but that he ran away." Frank's representative questioned them several times, "Did you say he ran out of there?" We responded, "Yeah, he did." Suddenly, the representative—the mob boss—screamed like a raging demon. "I told you to put him in the hospital. That means I want an emergency vehicle to scrape him up off the sidewalk," the boss yelled. At that particular moment, something changed in Frank's life. "Something in my heart changed," Frank acknowledged. "I saw the evil come out of this guy and the bloodthirstiness of these people."

That night Frank prayed and asked God to help him. He knew he needed to get out or he was going to die. A couple of days later, Frank checked himself into Long Island Teen Challenge. Frank testified,

"Teen Challenge completely changed my life. I denounced organized crime and that lifestyle and committed myself to the things of God." Frank describes the Teen Challenge program as a place of refuge. His life—previously bound by crime, drugs, paranoia, and rage—was free. Frank noted, "They said I was hopeless but I met others who had gone through the program that did a lot worse things than me, and their lives were changed. As long as a person has breath, there is hope. Teen Challenge says no one is hopeless."

After graduating, Frank continued to work as a staff member at the program. "I felt a call into ministry, but God was directing me to open up my own business," Frank remarked. "I told God I wanted to be in ministry. God said, you will be in ministry but as an owner of a business." Today, Frank is the president of a successful company called Brooklyn Elevator. "Here I am, a former 'coke head', now being able to financially bless drug rehab ministries like Teen Challenge through my business," Frank testified. He hopes to continue to support ministries that have to raise their support. "I hated to see the guys in the program go out and raise their own funds," Frank said. "I want people to understand that Teen Challenge changes lives and the guys shouldn't have to go out and raise their own money." Frank financially supports both Long Island and Brooklyn Teen Challenge and hopes to continue to be used by God to bless others.

Frank lives out a very different life from his former one. He not only ministers through his business but he is active in his church and teaches Celebrate Recovery to help those struggling with addiction. He laughs at where his life has taken him and remarks, "I have even done a political march in my hometown of Brooklyn. Me, a former wannabe crime gangster, on the front lines marching against opioids and pharmaceutical companies." It's like a mob movie with a twist where it ends with God bringing victory to Frank's life.

◇◇◇

A SONG FOR RYAN
Christina Palombi / Brooklyn Teen Challenge graduate (2016)

At twenty years old, Christina Palombi found herself pregnant for the second time. Almost one year after ending her first pregnancy in abortion, Christina was struggling with knowing what to do about this life growing inside her. It wasn't the question of her wanting a child. Ever since Christina was a young girl, she dreamed of having children and even adopting. But the reality of her situation was that Christina was a drug addict.

Her life up to this point played out like a tragic novel. Much of the family's time was spent in casinos where Christina remembers hours alone in front of the television: a substitute babysitter. By the age of 7, Christina was molested and forced to watch pornography which led to an ongoing addiction to porn. "I was told that was love," she remembers. "That abuse drove me to a physical need for the wrong type of affection and comfort." In her adolescent years, she began experimenting with cigarettes, marijuana, alcohol, and the drug Ecstasy. Christina would fill a Gatorade bottle with half water, half vodka and bring it to school.

Both home and school were volatile environments for Christina. Although she achieved average grades in school and was active in sports, she was often bullied and did not make friends easily. On the first day of her freshmen year, she got into a fight with another student. This seemed to stop the bullying. "Everyone seemed to back off of me," Christian recalled. "But this was dangerous because this became my mentality. I became a very mean-spirited person, but it was a defense mechanism to protect myself."

By sixteen, her parents went through a messy divorce, and Christina was passed back and forth between homes. The separation led to bouts of dark depression and her first rehab stint for an addiction to alcohol and marijuana. She tried to start fresh and stay sober, but her depression continued. "I began to be suicidal, and they put me on medication. I was so angry and depressed and wouldn't let anyone touch or hug me," she recalls. "I felt very alone and a burden to other people." After high school graduation and moving out of the house, Christina's addiction escalated. She began to depend more on alcohol, marijuana, ecstasy and was prescribed amphetamines.

With a growing dependency on drugs and battling depression, Christina had to make a choice about her pregnancy. It was here that God intervened in not only Christina's life but in the life of her son. "I almost got an abortion again, but someone told me about Jesus," she remembers. It was during this time that she visited a local chapel and watched as people were happily singing and worshipping God. "I didn't understand what they were doing, but I saw how happy they were," Christina remembers. "I made two decisions that day. First to not have an abortion, and secondly to learn more about God and the Bible." Christina was drug-free during her pregnancy and gave birth to a healthy baby boy named Ryan.

Unfortunately, Christina's struggles continued after experiencing severe post-partum depression and doctors prescribed more medication. Christina looked at her perfect son and thought she would never be a good enough mother for him. "I tried to be a good mom, but I didn't know how. I began to lean on drugs even more," she recalls. Christina was taking a large number of prescription drugs while trying to work two jobs. "Looking back, I don't know how I was even functioning," Christina remarked. Eventually Ryan's grandparents (the birth father's parents) took Ryan in while Christina moved through life with her addictions.

As an addict, Christina found it was easy to attract the same broken people who found themselves in her same situation. Friends would be open about their addictions and pain, and this led to Christina's introduction to more drugs. "It is so easy when you are already broken to get to the place of addiction and dependency," noted Christina. "A friend knows a friend who can get you different drugs and before you know it you're taking cocaine."

Then at age twenty-five years old, Christina met a man who was struggling with a heroin addiction. This relationship led to her 30 bag-a-day heroin habit. "We were desperate and obsessed with our addiction," Christina sadly remembered. "We were homeless together and broken. A codependent and destructive relationship." On Valentine's Day 2015, Christina's boyfriend overdosed in front of her in their motel room. His body was lifeless and blue. She dragged him across the floor, put him in in the bathtub, and tried to revive him by punching him in the chest and face. He finally woke up. "All I could think was I don't want to get caught. I am not done with my addiction," she regretfully admitted.

That was the beginning of Christina's breaking point. It spiraled her out of control for several more weeks where she described that time as "full-blown addiction." She couldn't hold down a job, wasn't visiting her son, and was stealing from family members and selling heroin to support her drug habit. Then on March 17, 2015, Christina was pulled over and arrested for drug possession. There were 69 bags of heroin in her car with 19 bags that she had injected before the arrest.

Christina's father visited her in jail and pleaded with her to enter a rehabilitation center. She looked at her dad and said, "No rehab is ever going to work with me. Right now, all I can think of is how beautiful your veins are and how awesome it would be to shoot heroin into your arm." It was one of the most disgusting remarks a daughter could say to a parent. Her dad broke down in tears looking at Christina through the glass partition and said, "Then I need you to write a letter to Ryan and explain to him that you are choosing drugs over him and you are going to die." It was those desperate words of a father and Christina's tragic reality that helped her decide to get help. "I did want to be a mom to my son," she admitted.

That Easter Sunday Christina attended church and walked up to the altar and accepted Jesus Christ into her life. She entered Brooklyn Teen Challenge ready to get help but filled with anger and rage. "The girls in the program thought I was demon possessed. I would punch the air in anger. I was challenging to handle; crying one minute and then angry and wanting to hit someone the next," Christina recalled. "They didn't like me, and my unpredictable behavior was probably the reason." Christina tried to run away several times but her breakthrough moment was when one of the staff leaders lovingly reprimanded her. Christina had never experienced discipline with love. "I grew up with people screaming at me and hitting me, or someone was afraid of me because I was screaming," she noted. "Nobody had taken authority over me with love. Nobody!"

Suddenly, Christina realized Teen Challenge was the place she needed to be. She read 1 John 4:18: "There is no fear in love. But perfect love drives out fear because fear has to do with punishment. The one who fears is not made perfect in love." She testified, "I began to cry because everything I knew about love was a lie. I knew nothing. I was very broken and what these people were telling me was true." Christina completely changed her attitude becoming an obedient resident in the program. "I had this zeal to learn more about God, and I wanted to feel this love that was expelling all my fear," she stated.

There were continuous highs and lows in the program for Christina with some breakthrough moments. One particular day, Christina was spending time in prayer and felt brokenness and healing over her abortion. "I felt God speak to me that He had delivered my baby to heaven. I was crying. There was so much healing happening. The shame and pain I was holding for that abortion, it was gone," Christina rejoiced. "I believe I will see my baby in heaven. I believe she is a girl and I named her Abigail." Fittingly, the Hebrew name means Father's joy. It was that point in her rehabilitation that Christina could visualize her future. She would help other women turn away from abortion so that they didn't have to experience that kind of grief and pain.

It was a long recovery period for Christina. A year program took her 16 months to complete. During that time she was able to visit with her son with the goal that one day Ryan would live with her full-time. She endured a custody battle over Ryan where the Judge restored all her rights due to the positive change in Christina's life.

The transition out of Teen Challenge hasn't been easy, and Christina will admit her struggles, but her life is drug-free with a new purpose. Her most significant change after Teen Challenge is her attitude towards life. Christina exclaimed, "Oh, I am full of joy now! I have peace in my life. Anger still gets the best of me at times, but I have learned it is okay to have emotions. It's what I do with those emotions that matter. My faith carries me through my struggles, and it makes me realize I can't do life on my own without God."

Christina has a new song in her heart both figuratively and literally. She writes music and sings. Recently she was given the opportunity to write worship music and take vocal and guitar lessons. "I have a huge desire to sing, and none of this would have been possible without Teen Challenge," she stated. "I chose my own path, but now God is restoring my original dreams of singing and being a mother." Today Christina is facing each day by faith. Her song lyrics reflect her healing and the life God has restored between a mother and her son.

Before he formed you in my womb
He set you apart
He knew all that would happen
He knows your heart...

But I want you to know
You're not fatherless
God loves you more than
What I could confess
Feeling my heart beating with yours
Mine skips a beat every time that yours does
I feel your pain our souls are connected
The choices I made have left you affected
I walked a path I don't want you to follow
I want you to have a better tomorrow
And I want you to know
You're not fatherless

HOPE PERSONIFIED
Bobby Lloyd / Brooklyn Teen Challenge (1984)

Humble, soft-spoken, a loving father, and a man of God are just a few of the words that characterize Bobby Lloyd. If you ask him what his life's calling is, he won't hesitate to answer, "The call of my life is to protect women, children, and families against the sexualized culture we live in." He's a man you want in your community. But what Bobby would also want you to know is that he's a changed man who once was a violent threat to his neighborhood.

Robert Lloyd was born in 1945 in a predominately black community of Long Island, New York. It bordered the affluent white neighborhood of Rockville Centre. There was racial tension between the two communities in the wake of the Civil Rights Movement. During his teen years, Bobby witnessed racial injustice, and this seemed to develop a defense mechanism in him as both a protector and a fighter. He didn't hesitate to defend his younger brother in school fights, punching kids with such force that it gave Bobby a reputation; "you don't mess with Bobby Lloyd."

Bobby's fighting instinct carried on throughout his teen years getting him mixed up in all the wrong circumstances. He had his first arrest at sixteen years old and then again at eighteen. Anger started to dictate his actions, and although he would protect those he loved, he would find himself in violent situations claiming self-defense or self-survival.

His teen years were also a time when he became addicted to pornography and was sexually active, eventually fathering three daughters by two different young ladies. By the time Bobby reached his twenties, he had a reputation as a "player" not being able to commit to any woman for an extended period. Eventually, Bobby fathered five daughters from three different women. His appetite for sex and violence was characterizing him in the neighborhood, but it would be drugs that would dictate his future.

At twenty-four years old, Bobby had his first encounter with heroin, first snorting it and then dealing it. Bobby worked as a local auto mechanic but soon ran with a drug dealer acting as his bodyguard. He quickly realized the financial advantages from selling drugs despite the risks. It wasn't long before Bobby was a big league drug dealer with a trusted circle of bodyguards and suppliers. He simultaneously became a heroin user and a dealer, selling drugs throughout Queens and Long Island.

During the 1970's, Bobby was a drug lord driving his black Cadillac and pristinely dressed in his polyester suits and fedora hat. His suit jacket would conceal his .38 revolver. Bobby had built up his drug cartel, and it wasn't long before the Italian Mafia, the most prominent drug players in the city, called on him knowing his influence in the drug business. He joined ranks with an Italian crime family. This opportunity led to more money and influence all across the metro area but with extreme risks. The Drug Enforcement Agency (DEA) now had Bobby on their radar.

Bobby was now constantly watching his back and fearful of the cops and the DEA. He couldn't afford to get sloppy in his drug dealings. But the combination of his drug use and his violent rage began to spiral his life out of control. Law enforcement had Bobby and his crew under surveillance. The DEA soon realized they were dealing with a major drug ring funneling large amounts of heroin. After months of investigation, on April 15, 1976, Bobby and eight members of his crew were arrested for conspiracy to sell narcotics. It was a huge drug bust for law enforcement.

On December 1, 1976, Bobby Lloyd stood before a Judge for his sentencing. He was guilty of conspiracy to sell and distribute narcotics and was sentenced to 2 ½ years to life in prison. His only possibility of release was the fact that his sentence was termed "2 ½ years to"; affording him the possibility of parole. Bobby was remanded to Sing Sing Correctional Facility, a notorious prison known for its infamous inhabitants of murderers and high-profile gangsters.

Somehow Bobby survived Sing Sing and was later transferred to Woodbourne prison. Then in December 1978, Bobby was released on a lifetime parole due to an experimental release program sanctioned by the state of New York. Bobby was a free man and eager to get his drug operation up and running again, but God had other plans for his life.

Dianne Jack was a family friend of Bobby Lloyd since he was a young boy. The Jack family were one of the few white families who stood up to the racial injustice of the 1960's in their community. Bobby would often hang out with Dianne's brothers. She was smitten with Bobby at a very young age, but it wasn't until after his prison release that Dianne and Bobby pursued a relationship. Dianne overcame a heroin addiction through a recovery program and faith in Jesus Christ. She was living drug-free and wanted Bobby to experience the same freedom, knowing the dramatic change it would have in his life. They continued their relationship, and Dianne prayed for Bobby's salvation. They married in the fall of 1979.

Bobby's life teetered between his criminal activity and attending church with Dianne. He was getting more involved with drugs, violence, and the old ways that previously put him in prison. One Sunday he had a dilemma. He promised to attend church with Dianne, but there was a drug pick-up he was supposed to make. Dianne was insistent that he keep his promise of spending Sundays with her. He conceded and asked his partner to go in his place with a couple of guys. That night, the drug deal went bad, and there was a shoot-out. The man in the passenger seat of the car was shot dead. Had Bobby gone out to do the drug pick-up, he would have been sitting in the passenger seat. Dianne's prayers and her relentless pursuit of their marriage saved Bobby's life.

There was no doubt that God intervened miraculously sparing Bobby's life. He committed his life to God and decided to stop selling drugs. However, he soon realized he couldn't quit his heroin habit and had to admit to his drug addiction. In February 1984, Bobby entered Brooklyn Teen Challenge at the age of thirty-eight. He walked into the program with life-controlling problems of sex and drug addiction. He was a man full of pride, resentment, and anger. Teen Challenge counseled Bobby through the Scriptures to put God first in his life. The program not only helped his addictions but it transformed his character. He graduated with a new life in Christ. He was the not the same man who had terrorized his neighborhood. His commitment to Christ and submitting to the authority of the Holy Spirit broke the walls of pride, anger, and injustice that Bobby had let build inside his heart for years.

Today, Bobby and Dianne Lloyd are living examples of the hope and freedom of Jesus Christ. They have raised a family of eight children including five daughters, three sons and now a total of sixteen grandchildren. A family of different ethnicities with four different fathers and five different mothers. They are a testament to the beauty of the family of God.

In 1989, Bobby helped to pioneer Long Island's first Teen Challenge program along with Dianne's brother, Jimmy Jack. Then miraculously in 1991, because of Bobby's work with at risk youth and the Teen Challenge ministry, Governor Andrew Cuomo granted him a pardon from his lifetime parole.

Perhaps, the most significant achievement in Bobby's life has been his calling to protect women, children, and families. In 1993, Bobby became the Executive Director of Long Island Citizens for Community Values (LICCV), an organization that fights to protect communities from the harmful effects of pornography and sexual violence through education awareness, campaigns, assisting government agencies with legislation, and mobilizing neighborhoods to protect their citizens from sexually oriented businesses.

For twenty-five years, LICCV has been instrumental in passing laws that protect women and children. Bobby has met with politicians, attorneys, company CEOs, and even the United States Attorney General in his commitment to making sure federal obscenity laws are enforced to protect communities. LICCV has helped to restore hundreds of women, children, men, and families from the devastating effects of sexual violence and pornography. Their goal is to help people live healthy lives.

In 2007, Bobby Lloyd was presented with the Excelsior Award by the state of New York. It is the highest award given to an individual for work done on behalf of the State. A former convicted gangster who ran one of the largest drug rings in the city, recognized for his honorable work. A man once bound by pornography, sex addiction, and violence now fighting against the very thing that was destroying his life. What a testimony!

Most of Bobby's friends from his days on the street have died. He has no doubt that had he not walked through the doors of Teen Challenge and learned how to live a new life in Christ; he would have either been dead or sentenced to life in prison. He testifies, "Jesus did not have to go to the cross, but he did because he loves me and that is why I am alive today. I think I am successful in what God is calling me to do. My kids can look at me and say they are proud of me. I am a lover of God who is trying to do God's will." Bobby Lloyd is another example of hope personified by the grace of God.

*This testimony was taken by permission from the book, *Black Night* by Bobby Lloyd with Steve Gallagher. Olive Press Messianic and Christian Publisher.

◇◇

THE TEEN CHALLENGE MANTLE
Jimmy Jack / Brooklyn Teen Challenge (1985)

In 1958, the same year that David Wilkerson traveled to New York City to minister to the gangs, a boy named Jimmy Jack was born in Long Island, New York. This date correlation is significant because of its proof that God will raise up the most unlikely people to further His kingdom. Jimmy's story is evidence that the legacy of Teen Challenge was meant to be carried on by those who found the hope of Jesus Christ through its doors.

Jimmy was the ninth and last child born into the Jack family including five daughters and four sons. When Jimmy was two-years-old, the Jacks moved to Rockville Centre, a predominately white neighborhood surrounded by African-American and Hispanic communities. During the 1960's Civil Right Movement, Jimmy's parents fought against racial inequality. Adele (Mama) Jack joined the movement and protested in her community for equal rights. The Jack family embraced people in need and opened their home to anyone no matter the color of their skin. "I was raised to love all people," Jimmy acknowledged.

The Jack children became friends with Black and Hispanic neighborhood kids. As the kids grew up, they dated and even married inter-racially. This full Scottish family was standing up against oppression by practicing racial justice in their home. Many in the white community rejected their openness to racial equality and labeled them "white trash." White families would not allow their children to play with the Jack kids. So Jimmy and his siblings found friendships with African-American families who would become lasting friends throughout their lives.

Despite the racial unity and compassion that Jimmy's parents embraced, there was a breakdown going on behind the walls of their home. It began with Jimmy's father. Alexander Hugh Jack was a World War II veteran. He was a tail gunner on a B-17 Bomber that was shot down over Brussels, Belgium. He was captured by the Nazis on March 2, 1944, and was a prisoner of war for fourteen months. After liberation, he received an honorable discharge, but the experiences of the War and the POW Camp eventually led to a mental breakdown.

Jimmy remembers his dad admitted to various psychiatric hospitals. The traumatic memories of the war led to bouts of depression and a violent temper. Psychiatrists prescribed anti-depressants for Alexander Hugh Jack. The demands of home and her husband's depression eventually led to Mama Jack's mental breakdown. She too was in and out of psychiatric hospitals. Both parents were prescribed unlimited amounts of valium, and other psychotropic drugs leaving them often sedated and comatose. The children were often without proper authority or parental guidance.

The Jack household was like a war zone, and from an early age Jimmy began to act out this pain and turmoil. By the age of ten, Jimmy started to smoke marijuana. He and his best friend Billy would get high and party with other neighborhood kids. They would spend their days like most boys playing basketball or other sports but partying became a focus of their lives. Jimmy and Billy would look for new hangouts. Alcohol, drugs, and sex consumed their adolescent and teen years. At the age of 13, Jimmy found out his girlfriend was pregnant, and she had an abortion. His promiscuity continued with more pregnancies that would end in abortion. Jimmy was always in search of love and security and would dull his pain using both drugs and girls.

Jimmy remembers his drug-crazed life. "With my parents heavily sedated, my house was a dope fiend's dream; we ate pills like candy. Some days each bedroom in our house had its own little party going on. I would sneak in and steal pills, acid, cocaine, and bags of pot from my brother's room and then share it with my friends," he recalled. "We sometimes had 50 to 100 people partying throughout our house. The police frequently came to check on our neighbor's complaints. My parents never knew because they were strung out on prescription drugs."

By the time Jimmy graduated from high school, his desire to get high was overshadowing everything else in his life. He had strong athletic skills, especially in basketball, but partying was his priority. Jimmy recalls with regret, "Looking back, it is hard to imagine how much I could have achieved both academically and athletically without the dulling effects and powerful influence of drugs and alcohol."

For the next several years, Jimmy's life was in a continuous downward spiral. He was arrested multiple times, couldn't keep a job, was frequently evicted from various apartments, and hustling on the streets consumed his days. Then suddenly, a near-death experience completely changed Jimmy's life. He watched Billy—his best friend since 5th grade—overdose. They had traveled to Manhattan to purchase four bags of heroin. Jimmy snorted the first bag, and then they cooked the other three so Billy could shoot it into his veins. Within seconds, Billy fell to the ground turning blue and unable to breathe. He had injected a lethal, uncut, and pure batch of heroin into his body.

"God, please! Don't let him die!" Jimmy cried. Billy was like a brother. He was family. Jimmy watched as paramedics tried to revive Billy's lifeless body. "I began to bargain with God. I promised Him that I would do anything He wanted me to. I would stop smoking. I would never drink again. I promised I would never do drugs again or steal again," Jimmy recalls. After several minutes of reviving Billy, paramedics looked at Jimmy. It was hopeless. Jimmy pleaded in sheer desperation, "I'll become whatever You want me to be, God. Just don't let Billy die!"

Miraculously, God answered Jimmy's prayer. He vividly recalls the miracle, "Suddenly Billy's life came back. He resurrected and jumped out of the ambulance. I ran up to Billy, hugged him, and we cried together." Jimmy trembled over what took place and suddenly became aware of the presence of God. He realized the depravity of his life and how God revealed His power through that terrifying experience. His life had to change.

On November 4, 1984, at twenty-six years old, Jimmy walked through the doors of Teen Challenge. He was ready to surrender his life to God. Kneeling down on a folding chair, he cried out again in prayer, "I commit my heart, soul, and life to the lordship of Jesus Christ! I'm clean! I'm clean! I'm clean!" Jimmy's new freedom in Christ completely changed his whole perspective and future for his life. He rejoiced in his new freedom, "The greatest revelation exploded in my heart when I realized God had saved me for a purpose." Before, Jimmy had no future. It was just day to day survival dulling his pain through drugs, alcohol, and women. He acknowledged his changed life, "Life was about purpose and restoring broken dreams. I knew God had a specific destiny for me. Suddenly, I had a burning desire to press on to embrace everything God had for my future."

Teen Challenge became a home of restoration and transformation for Jimmy. He remarked with affection, "When I came to Teen Challenge, they gave me a bed and a dresser. It was my home. My life was destroyed. I lost my home. Teen Challenge was everything I needed: a home, discipline, structure, love, and belongingness. You felt a part of this family, and then God provides the healing."

During Jimmy's recovery in Teen Challenge, he was granted permission to go home and marry Miriam, his girlfriend of seven years. Both he and Miriam had been through the struggle of drug addiction. Together, they committed to Christ and each other. Jimmy and Miriam entered Teen Challenge's family ministry where together they learned how to walk in their new freedom and faith in Jesus Christ. Jimmy's hopes and dreams were restored.

After Teen Challenge, Jimmy and Miriam attended Central Bible College in Missouri. Miriam received her degree in Christian Education, and Jimmy received his Bachelor of Arts in Bible Studies. In 1991, they traveled back to New York with a commission by Don Wilkerson to start the first Teen Challenge program in Long Island.

Since 1991, Jimmy and Miriam Jack have been living out the ministry God has called them to. They are the founders of Long Island Teen Challenge that has been helping those with life-controlling problems for over twenty-five years. Jimmy began Teen Challenge centers in Albany and Rochester, New York and in the Dominican Republic. Miriam and Jimmy are the pastors of Freedom Chapel in Amityville, New York. Jimmy is a pastor but an evangelist at heart. His ministries include coffee house outreaches, evangelism crusades, street ministries, and at-risk programs for children and those in need. He has taken the compassion, and racial unity instilled by his parents and is using it in ministry reaching people for Christ.

Jimmy and Miriam are parents to three children and one grandchild. They are a family living out the promises of God. They also rejoice over the testimony that nearly fifty family members of the extended Jack family have found hope through a Teen Challenge program. A home and family once broken by mental illness and drug addiction celebrates the victory of God's transforming power in their lives. Jimmy knows that God can restore anyone from drug addiction through various programs, but his family needed Teen Challenge. "My family needed more than an AA program, more than a church, or a recovery/detox center. We needed a long-term life-changing program that would drain the junk out and fill us with the power of God," Jimmy testified.

Today, Jimmy is president of New York Teen Challenge working alongside Don Wilkerson as President Emeritus. In Christian ministry, the word mantle is frequently referenced along with the word vision or God's calling. A mantle was a cloak word by Old Testament prophets, men distinguished to carry out the ministry of God. Today, we might not distinguish pastors or Christian leaders with mantles, but God still chooses men and women with specific burdens and for unique ministry purposes. Jimmy Jack wears the mantle of Teen Challenge. It is a part of his spiritual DNA. He carries out the same calling of David Wilkerson as a visionary and an evangelist. He also has the heart of a pastor like Don Wilkerson for the burdens and struggles of the lost and hurting. Don remarks about Jimmy, "He always acts like a student to a teacher with me, though he is a leader in his own right. Jimmy seems ordained for Teen Challenge from the spiritual womb." But what makes Jimmy uniquely qualified to carry this vision—like so many other leaders— is that he is a living testimony of the hope of Jesus Christ found through the ministry of Teen Challenge.

*This testimony was taken by permission from the book, *I Can Dream Again* by Jimmy Jack. Jimmy Jack Ministries and Freedom Publishing 2007.

Afterword

During the period of writing this book, I typed on a small makeshift desk next to a window overlooking a pear tree in my yard. The tree is quite large and strong. As I wrote each chapter, I noticed how the tree changed in all the various seasons. The very best view is always in late March or early April when the tree is full of many beautiful white blossoms that cover the tree in a soft white hue.

When I started this section of the book with my conclusion, that tree became the perfect symbol for why I wrote this story. Throughout my life, I would often be asked, "What was it like being raised in a ministry like Teen Challenge?" It was often a difficult question for me to answer as a child or a young adult. You don't often contemplate your life's upbringing when that is your norm.

But that tree and my view out my window became the answer to that question. Now as an adult with three children of my own, I can reflect on my upbringing. Being raised in the ministry of Teen Challenge was very similar to viewing that beautiful tree. I had the privilege of watching the growth of something that made a significant impact on my life.

I am grateful for my uncle and his obedience to God's leading on his life to plant the seed that began the ministry of Teen Challenge. My regret is that he is not alive today to read this story in his honor.

I am proud of my family's spiritual heritage and my parents who devoted their lives to establish the strong roots of a ministry that was not only able to grow but spread throughout the world.

I have great respect for all those who pioneered this ministry. Their service and dedication to the development of Teen Challenge has paved the way for the next generation.

I am humbled as I think of the many people and testimonies that have branched out of the program. My life was impacted by those who walked through the doors of Teen Challenge. Their changed lives reflected the love of Christ, and my heart was drawn to serve God because of their life stories.

I will always appreciate that God allowed me to have a beautiful view of a ministry that has grown and blossomed into a miraculous blessing that has brought hope to so many lives, a ministry that is still in full bloom all around the world.

But I am also challenged. God hasn't called me just to be a bystander with a window view. As a follower of Christ, I too am called to bring the hope of Christ to the world around me. That calling may look different than the view I grew up with, as He calls each of us in individual ways. But my hope is that you are challenged, too. For when God breaks our hearts to help others He can do miraculous things through us. I know, I was a witness to many of those miracles.

I pray that faith, hope, and love abide in the place—the address— where God is calling you.

—Julie (Wilkerson) Klose

CONTACT INFORMATION
FOR ADULT AND TEEN CHALLENGE CENTERS

Brooklyn Teen Challenge
444 Clinton Avenue
Brooklyn, New York 11238
(718) 789-1414
www.brooklyntc.org

Global Teen Challenge
P.O. Box 511
Columbus, GA 31902
(706) 576-6555
www.globaltc.org

**Adult and Teen Challenge USA
(national office)**
5250 N Towne Center Drive
Ozark, Missouri 65721
(417) 581-2181
www.teenchallengeusa.com

Notes

1. National Institute on Drug Abuse-Overdose Death Rates- https://www.drugabuse.gov/related-topics/trendsstatistics/overdose-death-rates

2. Fox, Maggie. 2016. "Obama Seeks $1 Billion to Fight Drug Abuse." NBC News. February 2. http://www.nbcnews.com/health/health-news/obama-seeks-1-billion-fight-drug-abuse-n509816.

3. David Ingles Music. 1976

4. John, Book of. n.d. "Chapter 12, Verse 46 ."

5. Farmer, Katie. 2014. http://michaelfarmer.org/.

6. Life Magazine. 1957. "Teen-Age Burst of Brutality."

7. Davidson, Irwin D. 1959. The Jury is Still Out. New York: Harper and Brothers.

8. (Wilkerson 1962), 7. Wilkerson, David. 1962. The Cross and the Switchblade. New York: Jove Books.

9. (Wilkerson 1962), 19.

10. (Wilkerson 1962), 20.

11. (Davidson 1959), 132.

12. (Wilkerson 1962), 26.

13. (Wilkerson 1962), 26.

14. (Davidson 1959), 296.

15. (Bob Combs, God's Turf 1969), pg 14

16. (Davidson 1959), 303.

17. (Harris 2005), 33.

18. (Harris 2005), 43.

19. (Harris 2005), 88.

20. (G. Wilkerson 2014), 41. Wilkerson, Gary. 2014. The Cross, The Switchblade, And The Man Who Believed David Wilkerson . Grand Rapids, MI: Zondervan.

21. (Gary Wilkerson, The Cross, The Switchblade, And the Man who Believed: David Wilkerson 2014) pg 41 Zondervan

22. (Harris 2005), 84.

23. (Harris 2005), 84.

24. (Harris 2005), 85.

25. (D. Wilkerson 2002), 5. Wilkerson, Don. 2002. Called to the Other Side. Locust Grove, Virginia: Global Teen Challenge Publishing.

26. (D. Wilkerson 2002), 4.

27. (G. Wilkerson 2014), 69.

28. (D. Wilkerson, The Gutter and the Ghetto 1969), 9. —. 1969. The Gutter and the Ghetto. Waco, Texas: Word Books.

29. (D. Wilkerson, The Cross is Still Mightier Than The Switchblade 1996), 8.

30. (G. Wilkerson 2014), 84

31. (D. Wilkerson, The Cross is Still Mightier Than The Switchblade 1996), 12.

32. (D. Wilkerson, Called to the Other Side 2002), 31.

33. (D. Wilkerson, The Gutter and the Ghetto 1969), 11.

34. (D. Wilkerson, The Gutter and the Ghetto 1969), 13.

35. (D. Wilkerson, The Gutter and the Ghetto 1969), 18.
36. (D. Wilkerson, The Gutter and the Ghetto 1969), 20.
37. (D. Wilkerson 1962), 104.
38. (D. Wilkerson 1962), 105.
39. (D. Wilkerson 1962), 106.
40. (D. Wilkerson 1962), 108.
41. (D. Wilkerson 1962), 107.
42. (D. Wilkerson 1962), 109.
43. (D. Wilkerson 1962), 111.
44. (D. Wilkerson 1962), 140.
45. (John F. Kennedy Presidential Library and Museum 1962)
46. (D. Wilkerson, A Positive Cure for Drug Addiction n.d.)
47. (David Batty 2008), 20.
48. (D. Wilkerson, The Gutter and the Ghetto 1969), 25.
49. (D. Wilkerson, The Gutter and the Ghetto 1969), 26.
50. (D. Wilkerson, The Gutter and the Ghetto 1969), 28.
51. (Combs 1969), 89.
52. (D. Wilkerson, The Gutter and the Ghetto 1969), 35.
53. (D. Wilkerson, A Positive Cure for Drug Addiction n.d.)
54. (David Manuel, The Jesus Factor 1977), 7.
55. (Gary Wilkerson, David Wilkerson 2014), 97.
56. (David Manuel, The Jesus Factor 1977), 28.
57. (D. Wilkerson, The Gutter and the Ghetto 1969), 51.
58. Ibid, 51
59. Ibid, 51
60. (D. Wilkerson, The Gutter and the Ghetto 1969), 52.
61. Ibid, 40.
62. Ibid, 4.
63. Ibid, 54.
64. Ibid, 54.
65. Ibid, 61.
66. (Raul Gonzalez, Raul A True Story 1989), 133.
67. Ibid, 134.
68. (D. Wilkerson, The Cross is Still Mightier Than the Switchblade 1996), 70
69. Ibid, 70-71.
70. Ibid, 72.
71. (D. Wilkerson, The Cross is Still Mightier Than The Switchblade 1996), 81
72. (D. Wilkerson, The Gutter and the Ghetto 1969),70
73. Ibid, 79.
74. Ibid, 63.
75. Ibid, 52.
76. Ibid, 71.
77. Ibid, 71.
78. Ibid, 71.
79. Ibid, 71.
80. Ibid, 76.
81. Ibid, 72.
82. Ibid, 164.
83. Ibid, 164.
84. Ibid, 89.
85. Ibid, 90.
86. Ibid, 91.
87. (D.Wilkerson, The Gutter and the Ghetto 1969), 136
88. (D.Wilkerson, The Cross is Mightier Than the Switchblade), 73
89. (Archives) The Miracle School pamphlet.
90. (Don Wilkerson, Confessions of a Hope Pusher 2014), 142
91. (Harris, 2005), 167
92. (Kelly Minter, Ruth Bible Study-Life Way)

THE WILKERSON FAMILY,
1940'S (LEFT TO RIGHT:
RUTH, DAVID, KENNETH,
DON, AND JERRY)

THE WILKERSON FAMILY, 1950'S
FRONT ROW: RUTH, JERRY, DONALD
BACK ROW: DAVID, ANN,
KENNETH, JUANITA

KENNETH AND ANN
WILKERSON

Brother "Davie" and his Messerschmitt KR200
PLEASE REMEMBER ME IN YOUR PRAYERS

The HOUR OF DELIVERANCE
RADIO & TELEVISION

Brother "Davie" Wilkerson

"...the Prince of the world commeth and hath nothing in me..." (John 14:30)

DAVID'S EARLY
MINISTRY OUTREACH

MASS MURDER TRIAL

In a New York criminal court seven ninety-faced boys, aged 15 to 18 and dressed in their Sunday best, went on trial for their lives. On a hot night last summer in an uptown Manhattan park, a 15-year-old police victim named Michael Farmer had been beaten and stabbed to death by one of the teen-age gangs which have terrorized sections of the city. Charged with the murder are the boys above. Eleven others then under 15 years old, who were legally too young to be prosecuted, are in reform school.

The trial, which promises to be lengthy, is remarkable both for the age and number of defendants involved and for the number of defense attorneys—27 in all. Each boy has several lawyers, all of whom, including such eminent criminal lawyers as James D. C. Murray and Harold O. N. Frankel, were appointed by the court. They jam the small courtroom so tightly there seems barely room to try the case.

The prosecutor, Assistant District Attorney Robert Reynolds, began with testimony from 16-year-old Roger McShane (left). He and Farmer

IN COURTHOUSE 13, OF THE 27 DEFENSE LAWYERS GATHER BEFORE TRIAL.

OF A TEEN-AGE GANG

had gone to the park to take a furtive swim in the pool, which was closed for the night. There they were set upon by a gang armed with knives, metal pipes, dog chains and a machete. McShane, stabbed twice in the back, ran to safety. But Farmer, unable to run on his polio-weakened leg, was left dying in the grass.

The frightening, senseless reason for the attack was told by the second prosecution witness, Ralph Lago (right), member of a gang that called itself the Egyptian Dragons. Though one of the youngest (14) of the gang, Lago was their "war lord," responsible for plotting intergang battles. Bitter enemies of this gang were the Jesters who fought with the Egyptian Dragons over the public park pool, which each claimed as their territory. Then, on that summer night, 10 vengeful Dragons, some fortified with wine, lay in ambush for the Jesters near a place in the pool fence where aluminum swimmers had pried open a hole for easier entrance. The first boys to come were McShane and crippled Michael Farmer,

SESSION BEGINS. EACH OF THEM, AS A COURT APPOINTEE, WILL BE PAID SOME

LIFE MAGAZINE ARTICLE THAT
SPARKED DAVID'S MINISTRY IN
NEW YORK CITY, FEBRUARY 1958

THE FAMOUS PHOTO OF DAVID
TAKEN AT THE COURTHOUSE,
FEBRUARY 28, 1958

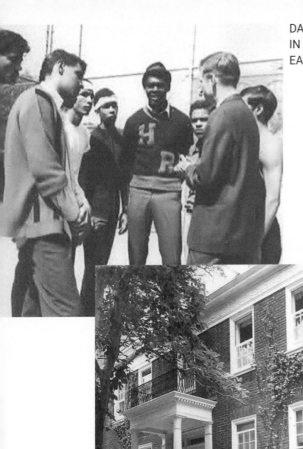

DAVID WITH THE BISHOP GANG
IN BROWNSVILLE, BROOKLYN,
EARLY 1960'S

416 CLINTON AVENUE—THE FIRST
TEEN CHALLENGE PROGRAM

DAVID AND HIS MOTHER ANN
WILKERSON WORKING AT 416

A TEEN CHALLENGE STREET RALLY IN THE EARLY
DAYS OF THE MINISTRY

TEEN CHALLENGE CHAPEL
AT CONEY ISLAND

DON AND CINDY WILKERSON ON
THE FRONT STEPS AT 416

ANN WILKERSON AND FAYE MIANULLI OUTSIDE THE LOST
COIN OUTREACH MINISTRY IN GREENWICH VILLAGE

444 CLINTON AVENUE- ADMINISTRATION BUILDING

THE TEEN CHALLENGE TRAINING CENTER
(THE FARM OR GOD'S MOUNTAIN)

RESIDENTS IN FRONT OF THE TEEN CHALLENGE
TRAINING CENTER, 1970'S

WALTER HOVING HOME
WOMEN'S CENTER

TEEN CHALLENGE
INSTITUTE OF MISSIONS IN
RHINEBECK, NEW YORK

DON WILKERSON REPRESENTING TEEN CHALLENGE
WITH PRESIDENT FORD, 1976

BROOKLYN TEEN CHALLENGE
HOPE LIVES HERE...
FREEDOM IS FOUND HERE...
CHANGED LIVES LEAVE HERE!

"Therefore, if anyone is in Christ, he is a new creation; old things have passed away; behold, all things have become new." 2 Cor. 5:17

A SIGN DISPLAYED AS YOU ENTER 416 MEN'S
PROGRAM, TODAY

DON AND DAVID WILKERSON IN THE 1970'S

TO VIEW MORE PHOTOS
GO TO INSTRAGRAM: GIVING_HOPE_AN_ADDRESS